Once-a-Month
COOKING

Once-a-Month COOKING

A proven system for spending less time

in the kitchen and enjoying delicious,

homemade meals everyday

MIMI WILSON AND MARY BETH LAGERBORG

BROADMAN
&HOLMAN
PUBLISHERS

Nashville, Tennessee

© 1986, 1992, 1999 by Mimi Wilson and Mary Beth Lagerborg
All rights reserved
Printed in the United States of America

0-8054-1835-0

Published by Broadman & Holman Publishers, Nashville, Tennessee
Editorial Team: Vicki Crumpton, Janis Whipple, Kim Overcash
Page Design: Paul T. Gant Art & Design
Typesetting: PerfecType, Nashville, Tennessee

Published in 1986 by St. Martin's Press. Second edition in 1992 published by
Focus on the Family Publishing. This book was originally published in 1982
under the title *Freeze and Save* and in 1984 as *Dinner's Ready*.

Dewey Decimal Classification: 641.5
Subject Heading: MAKE-AHEAD COOKERY / COOKING / FAMILY
Library of Congress Card Catalog Number: 98-40917

Unless otherwise stated all Scripture citation is from the NIV, the Holy Bible, New
International Version, copyright © 1973, 1978, 1984 by International Bible Society; other
versions include The Living Bible (TLB), copyright © 1971 by Tyndale House Publishers.

Library of Congress Cataloging-in-Publication Data

Wilson, Marilyn S., 1946–
    Once-a-month cooking / Marilyn S. Wilson, Mary E. Lagerborg.
        p. cm.
    Originally published: 1992.
    Includes index.
    ISBN 0-8054-1835-0 (pbk.)
    1. Make-ahead cookery. I. Lagerborg, Mary Beth. II. Title.
    TX652.W5647   1999
    641.5'55 — dc21

                                                            98-40917
                                                            CIP

9 10 11 12   05 04

Dedication

Our most expert—and honest—recipe testers

Calvin Wilson	Alex Lagerborg
Kurt and Lori Wilson	Tim Lagerborg
Tom and Kyndra Trinidad	Dan Lagerborg
Kevin Wilson	Andrew Lagerborg

Table of Contents

Acknowledgments

Our warmest thanks to family and friends who have contributed recipes, table talk questions, and their perspective to this edition of *Once-a-Month Cooking:*

Kurt Wilson
Lori Wilson
Renee Loring
Sue Herd
Cynthia Bahlman
Capt. Lois True
Ginger Brown
Linnea Rein
Sandi Hanson
Cala Doolittle
Marge Rodemer
Alice Tate

INTRODUCTION

$\mathcal{S}$irs," he said, "please don't go any further. Stop awhile and rest here in the shade of this tree while I get water to refresh your feet, and a bite to eat to strengthen you. Do stay awhile before continuing your journey."

Abraham, Genesis 18: 3–5, TLB

*W*hat's for dinner?" is the perennial, pesky question that draws you to this book. You might have tonight covered, but your family's need to eat—best yet eat together—comes in relentless waves.

And you have things to do besides cook! *Once-a-Month Cooking* is a method for people who don't always want to cook, but want to have cooked. You are smart and you understand that nothing unravels the seams of quality family time faster than having nothing on hand for dinner. Not having clean laundry runs a distant second.

Once-a-Month Cooking is a method of cooking a month's (or two weeks') dinner entrées at a time and freezing them. Yes, of course it works! (That's the question we're asked most often. Although a couple who cooks this way was featured in the *National Enquirer*, the method is not outrageous.)

You don't have to be particularly organized or a good cook to do this. You don't need a separate freezer. You don't need a Tupperware distributorship, although a drawerful of Tupperware will help.

We will take you by the hand and give you a shopping list and lots of direction. We'll tell you what size containers to freeze the food in and suggest what to serve with your entrées. When you're finished, gazing into your well-stocked freezer will be a near-spiritual experience. Afterward, on any given day you can cook from scratch if you want to, but if you don't have time—no problem. This is a great way to simplify your life, relieving it of the daily stress of what to fix for dinner.

The beauty of once-a-month cooking is that it provides the convenience of a home meal replacement—the restaurant industry's jargon for the take-out meal—with the aroma, appeal, taste, nutrition, and cost savings of home cooking. For the investment of one large grocery haul and a day of mega-cooking, you have a month's (or two weeks') entrées available on time each day with little effort on your part beyond putting an entrée into the oven and steaming vegetables or tossing a salad. And you won't need to dash in for fast food, Chinese takeout, or to the grocery store deli.

This system saves you money. Convenience foods are costly. So are forays into the supermarket at 5:00 P.M. with two preschoolers. A list that began with four items yields a cart holding twenty-two, including Fruit Loops and Big Chew gum. With once-a-month cooking you will have one large shopping trip a month (or two weeks), then shop perhaps once a week for fresh produce, breakfasts, and lunches.

A bonus from your day's cooking investment is your flexibility. Having guests is more fun when the main dish is ready in advance. Your family can carry on if you have surgery or a new baby, when the holidays approach, or if you are traveling. What a joy it is to be able to respond to special needs of your family and of others!

We all know that nutrition fares better when we aren't eating catch-as-catch-can. And if you or another family member are on a special diet, once-a-month cooking is an excellent way to feed the rest of the tribe.

You may want to try the two-week plan rather than a whole month if you are cooking in bulk for the first time or your family is small (fewer than four people). In that case two weeks' worth will last you at least three weeks if you package it in more, and smaller containers.

The greatest benefit of once-a-month cooking, however, is that it gives you a better shot at pulling the family together—at least a few evenings a week—to disengage from the concerns of the world and engage with one another. A warm meal on a set table wafts the aroma of care and value to a family. As one mom said, "When the food is ready, and we're gathered at the table, the rest of the craziness doesn't seem to matter."

Home meal replacements make it too easy for a family to separate, grab the meal when they want, and see to their own needs. *Once-a-Month Cooking* will help you have a meal to gather round. Share the kitchen chores as well as your mealtimes together.

Once we're at the table it's discouraging to fall into the same conversation ruts about work or teachers, or how a child has misbehaved today. With our own families and friends we've found it's helpful and fun to sometimes "put a question on the table." That is, ask a question that each person at the table must address, but for which there is no right or wrong answer, such as "What is the funniest thing you saw today?" "What is your favorite room of our home and why?" "If you were an animal rather than a person, what animal would you like to be?" We've included table talk questions to prime the pump for you. Turn off the television, ignore the telephone, and enjoy what you will learn about one another.

This cooking system was devised by Mimi to meet the daily needs of a busy family that had company often. In the years since then we have been encouraged and sometimes amused by the many uses people have found for—as we call it—"the method." Here are some that stretch beyond the obvious feeding of a busy family. Perhaps they will expand your vision for how you can use the wealth of food you will soon have on hand.

- Freeze individual portions to stock the freezer of an elderly parent or friend.
- Develop this as an at-home business to serve busy, two-income families. A day care provider uses *Once-a-Month Cooking* so that for a fee parents can pick up a dinner entrée with their child!
- Cook the method with friends in a church or community kitchen and use the entrées to take to families in crisis.
- For a baby gift or for a woman experiencing a difficult pregnancy, have the expectant mother purchase the groceries from the shopping list. The next day you come to her home, cook the entrées, and put them into her freezer.

We can't resist sharing our two personal favorite applications. On a visit to Peru, Mimi's husband, Calvin, a family physician, was part of a medical team that trekked into the jungle to treat a people group dying of pneumonia. When the team needed additional food, Mimi took frozen entrées, packaged in Tupperware and wrapped in newspapers, to a nearby airstrip. The pilot flew over the team's camp site in the jungle and dropped the entrées to them. We call this one "Bombs Away."

The final one involves a letter we received. We receive many letters (and phone calls on cooking day). Some users say the results have saved their marriages. One user said she actually accomplished cooking this way although her past cooking catastrophes had put a person in the hospital and included things like frying a chicken in Tide. This following letter is a favorite:

> Dear Madam,
> I ordered the book *Once-a-Month Cooking* . . . .
> As a bachelor, I have cooked in bulk for years, though my menu consists of only one or two items.
> I am interested in mail order bulk food distributors. Do you have some addresses I could try?
> Thanks for your time,
> Dave Listoe
> North Pole, Alaska

Whatever your impulse for trying *Once-a-Month Cooking*, we trust you'll find generous rewards for your day's cooking.

INTRODUCTION

If you have used a previous edition of *Once-a-Month Cooking*, you will find in this edition a new two-week cycle of recipes, a few recipe substitutions in the other menu cycles, and a general fine-tuning. You will also see that one two-week plan, chapter two, is a condensed version of a one-month cycle, so its recipes appear both places.

Are you ready to win the race to have meals on hand? On your mark. Get set. Let the adventure begin!

INTRODUCTION

CHAPTER ONE
Cooking the Once-a-Month Way

*C*heerfully share your home
with those who need a meal or a
place to stay for the night.

1 Peter 4:9, TLB

7

WARMING UP: AN OVERVIEW OF THE ONCE-A-MONTH PLAN

*T*his cooking method enables you to prepare either a month or two weeks' main dishes at once and freeze them. The book includes two choices of one-month cycles and three choices of two-week cycles. If you rotate among these, you can easily provide great mealtime variety. We suggest that you start with a cycle from the book to get used to the method. Then you can experiment with adding favorite family recipes. Turn to chapter 9 for help in adapting the method to your own recipes.

Each menu cycle gives you a menu calendar that shows the month's entrées at a glance, a grocery shopping list, a list of staples that the menu cycle assumes you have on hand (so you can buy any you don't have), a list of the containers you will need for freezing the entrées, step-by-step instructions for preparing the recipes in sequence on your cooking day, and finally the recipes themselves in the order you will prepare them.

To serve an entrée, you will need to thaw the dish and heat it. Meanwhile you can turn your attention to preparing a vegetable, salad, or perhaps a dessert to serve with it. The time-consuming preparation and cleanup is done all at once on your mega-cooking day!

Since many of the entrées can be frozen in freezer bags instead of bulkier hard-sided containers, even a month's cycle can be stored in the freezer accompanying your refrigerator. If you are using your refrigerator's freezer, you will need to make room in it by cleaning it out before your cooking day. (Sooner or later you would need to deal with those hard knots of leftovers anyway!) Right after cooking day you will not have room in the refrigerator's freezer for things like ice cream and loaves of bread, but as you use entrées from the freezer you can add these to it.

The recipes in *Once-a-Month Cooking* don't come from stainless-steel test kitchens, but have been tested numerous times in homes by cooks of various cooking abilities. We have selected recipes we think your family will eat and enjoy. They were chosen for taste, variety, nutritional value, easily available ingredients, and how well they lend themselves to freezing.

One of the two-week cycles consists entirely of low-fat entrées, selected in consultation with a dietitian. With the other menu cycles you may adjust as you like for low-fat, for example, using soups and dairy products with reduced fat content.

You will find that the recipes vary in serving size. The average is five or six servings. Some serve four; a few serve twelve. Depending upon the ages (and eating habits) of your children, if you have four or fewer family members, you may want to divide and freeze each larger-serving entrée in two or more meal-size portions. The largest recipes are great for serving company or ensuring leftovers the following day.

You may find that a month menu cycle actually feeds your family for five weeks or six or more — particularly if you occasionally eat out or supplement your menu with dinner salads or easy meals like grilled meats and vegetables.

In chapter 8 you will find a few of our favorite bread, breakfast, dessert, salad, and vegetable recipes to serve with your entrées.

Consult chapter 10 for helpful information on such things as freezing tips and food measurement equivalents.

AT THE STARTING LINE

Are you ready to cook? Or at least ready to *think* about getting ready to cook? Let us provide some tips to streamline the process.

First, read this introductory material. Then choose which menu cycle you would like to try this month and read through that chapter so you'll know what's ahead.

Next comes the hardest part: crossing off the time on your calendar to grocery shop and cook. But if you don't do this, you won't accomplish once-a-month cooking. These should be on adjacent days. Don't try to shop and cook on the same day, especially if you have young children, or you won't like us very much! You simply won't have the time or energy to do both. You might also not like us about four hours into your cooking day, when your feet are complaining and every pot and pan you own is dirty. But we are consoled by the thought that you will like us *very much* when you peek at your larder, carefully labeled and layered in your freezer, as well as each day thereafter at about 5:00 P.M. The month cycles require about (of course this varies with the cook) a nine-hour day. The two-week cycles take about four to five hours.

Cook with a friend or your spouse or an older child. The day goes so much more quickly when you divide the work and add the conversation. If you have young children, a cooking companion can help tend the kids, answer the phone, and wipe the counters. You can either divide up the food or cook one day a month at your friend's home and one day a month at your own.

Trust us that you will want to go out to dinner on cooking day. Yes, we know you will have plenty on hand for dinner, but you won't want to face any of it on your plate. This will pass. Go out, then have your spouse and kids wash the dishes.

Err to the side of buying a little more produce, chicken, and ground beef than is called for on your shopping lists. You can always use these for salads, soups, and sandwiches. If you have chicken broth left over, freeze it in an ice cube tray. When the cubes are frozen, pop them into a freezer bag. You can pull out a cube when a recipe calls for chicken broth, or make spur-of-the-moment chicken soup with leftovers.

You may want to photocopy the recipes and attach them to large index cards. In many cases you will be working on more than one recipe at a time. You can lay out your recipe cards in sequence to save you from having to keep turning the pages.

Don't even think about trying to do extra baking on your cooking day. If you enjoy making pie crust and want to use your own rather than a store-bought one, prepare the pie crust a couple of days ahead.

Finally, although you need to free yourself of commitments on your cooking day, the day will go much easier if you feel free to take a break to tend to the children's needs, make a phone call, or just sit down and rest! Wear supportive shoes. Listen to your favorite music. Crack open a kitchen window for ventilation and to let the good smells pour out.

The secret of the method involves *doing all similar processes at once:* browning ground beef and chopping onions and cooking chicken only once rather than several times a month. Imagine the hours this saves!

GROCERY SHOPPING HINTS

Before you go to the supermarket, read the grocery and staples lists for the menu cycle you plan to use. The staples list contains items you need but probably have on hand. Look through your cupboards and add the missing staple items to the grocery shopping list. Also check the list of suggested freezer containers to see if you need to buy any of them.

For added convenience, use a copier to reproduce the grocery list; then write in the other staple items or containers you'll need to buy. The grocery lists have been categorized by sections of food to help speed you through the store.

If you shop for a month menu cycle, you will have to push one cart and pull another. You may need to budget more carefully in order to set aside the funds needed to purchase food for all your dinner entrées at once. But keep in mind that over the course of the month you will save money on your food bill by cooking this way because you'll be buying in bulk, eating out less often, and eliminating unplanned trips to the supermarket.

Your shopping trip will take you a couple of hours, so don't try to wedge it between two appointments. If you take young children, be sure to go when everyone is well-fed and rested. It also helps to break up the trip. For example, go mid-morning to a discount food store to buy in bulk, have lunch at a favorite spot, and then finish any leftover shopping at the supermarket. If a friend or relative can baby-sit for you on shopping day, you will accomplish more in less time.

When you get home from shopping, you don't have to put everything away. Stack the canned goods and dry ingredients on a table or counter because you'll be using them soon. Keeping them within sight can inspire you for the task ahead!

The grocery shopping lists include some items with asterisks(*). These can be stored because you will not need them until the day you serve the corresponding entrée. Mark the labels of these items to remind you not to use them by mistake. For example, place an X in marker across a soup label, a package of rice or spaghetti, or on a plastic bag holding a fresh tomato.

THE DAY BEFORE COOKING DAY

After you've returned from the grocery store, clear off the kitchen counters, removing any appliances you won't be using. Create as much free countertop space as you can. Then, following the "Equipment Needed for Cooking Day" list, pull out your food processor, mixer, bowls—the tools you will need. If you have room, you may also want to get out the staple items.

Make sure you have all needed groceries on hand. Then perform the tasks that your chosen menu cycle outlines for the day before cooking day.

If you don't have a food processor to chop and slice the vegetables, you may want to cut them up the day before cooking since this is one of the most time-consuming tasks. Then store these vegetables in the refrigerator in cold water, inside tightly sealed plastic containers, or omit the water and seal them in zip-closure bags. (Do not store mushrooms in water.)

Finally, check the list of freezer containers needed for the entrées in your menu cycle and get out the ones you'll need. You can usually store entrées in freezer bags unless they are layered, like lasagna, or contain a lot of liquid. Food stored in freezer bags can be thawed in the bag and then warmed in a suitable container.

COOKING THE ONCE-A-MONTH WAY

CHAPTER ONE

COOKING DAY

The assembly order for each menu cycle is a step-by-step guide to preparing all your entrées. Read through the assembly order before you start to cook. Since you will usually be working on more than one recipe at a time, getting an overview will give you a sense of how the steps flow together.

The following suggestions will help make this method work best for you:

✽ Place an empty trash can in the center of the kitchen, and corral the pets where they won't be underfoot. You'll want to avoid wasted motion wherever possible on cooking day.

✽ Use a timer—or two timers when necessary—to remind you something is in the oven or boiling for a certain length of time.

✽ Pause to wash pots and pans as necessary. Washing dishes and wiping up periodically as you work will help you work more efficiently and make end-of-the-day cleanup easier.

✽ If you sauté several food items in succession, use the same skillet. Sometimes you'll only need to wipe it out and put in the next ingredients. Put a slow cooker to work by using it overnight for brisket, for example, and then for soup or stew on cooking day.

✽ Set frequently used spices along the back of the stove or on a nearby counter. Use one set of measuring cups and spoons for wet ingredients and another for dry. That way you'll need to wash them less often.

✽ You will *perform all similar tasks at once.* For example, grate, chop, and slice all the carrots, celery, cheese, and onions. Set them aside in separate bowls or plastic bags. Cook all the chicken if you didn't do that the day before. Brown all the ground beef and sauté all the onions at one time. These tasks may seem tedious, but you will have accomplished a lot when you're finished, and assembling the dishes will go much faster.

✽ Whenever a chicken recipe doesn't specifically call for cooked chicken in the ingredients list, it means you will use raw chicken.

✽ At the close of your cooking day, save leftover sliced or diced vegetables and cooked meat for a soup, a salad, or for snacks.

FOOD STORAGE AND FREEZER TIPS

As you complete recipes, set them aside on a table to cool enough so they won't heat up the other foods in your freezer. When one or two have cooled, label each with the name of the entrée, the date you prepared it, and cooking instructions, so you won't have to consult the recipe when you are preparing to serve it. For example:

Aztec Quiche

10/8

Bake uncov. 40–50 mins. at 325 degrees

If a recipe calls for cheese to be sprinkled on top the last few minutes of baking, pour the grated cheese in a small freezer bag. Tape the bag to the side or top of the corresponding entrée's container so that you are freezing the two together.

Make the best use of your 13x9x2-inch baking dishes. Spray a dish with nonstick spray, line the dish with heavy aluminum foil, seal the entrée, and freeze it. When the entrée has frozen completely, remove it in the foil and return it to the freezer, thereby freeing your dish to be used for something else.

When sealing food for freezing, remove as much air from the container as possible, and seal it airtight. That will help guard against the cardboard-like taste called "freezer burn." When using freezer bags, label the bag with an indelible marker before you insert the food.

Post the menu of foods you've prepared on your freezer or inside a cupboard door to help you choose each day's dinner and to keep an inventory of what entrées you've used. Check off the dishes as you serve them. For the freshest taste, seal containers airtight and use them within a month to six weeks. (For additional freezer storage tips, see chapter 10.)

SERVING SUGGESTIONS

Remember each evening to pull the next night's entrée from the freezer and put it in the refrigerator to thaw. If the food is in a freezer bag, set the bag in a casserole dish to thaw, in case any liquid leaks out. You can also thaw the dish in the microwave the next day. If the entrée is sealed securely in a freezer bag, you can thaw it in cold water. We don't recommend that you thaw food on the counter because of the danger of spoilage if it sits out too long after it is thawed.

Each recipe includes suggestions for salads or vegetables you might serve with the entrée. You'll find some of those recipes in chapter 8. Now that you've saved time on your entrées, try some new salads, vegetables, or desserts, whether you'll have company or the same familiar faces around your table.

You'll spend less time in the kitchen during the coming weeks. You will save time, money, and energy that you can invest in many other ways. Imagine how good it will feel to

COOKING THE ONCE-A-MONTH WAY

have entrées on hand, and to have an immediate answer to each day's nagging question: "What's for dinner?"

Let's get cooking!

EQUIPMENT NEEDED FOR COOKING DAY

On cooking day, you'll want to reuse bowls and pans as much as possible to conserve counter and stove-top space. The following equipment will be needed:

APPLIANCES

blender or hand mixer (one-month A plan)
Crockpot (one-month A and B plans)
food processor or grater

POTS, PANS, AND SKILLETS

1 extra large pot, canning kettle, or 2 large pots
1 large saucepan with lid
1 medium saucepan with lid
1 small saucepan
1 large skillet
1 medium skillet
1 rimmed baking sheet (two-week A plan, one-month B plan); 2 rimmed baking sheets (low-fat plan)

BOWLS AND CONTAINERS

1 set of large, medium, and small mixing bowls
8 to 12 small-to-medium bowls or plastic bags (for grated, sliced, or chopped ingredients)

MISCELLANEOUS TOOLS

can opener
colander
cutting board
hot pads

kitchen scissors

knives (cutting and paring)

ladle

2 sets of measuring cups (one for wet ingredients and one for dry)

2 sets of measuring spoons (one for wet ingredients and one for dry)

masking tape or labels

metal or plastic serving spatula

mixing spoons

rolling pin

rubber gloves (for deboning chicken and mixing food)

rubber spatula

tongs

vegetable peeler

waterproof marking pen

wire whisk

CHAPTER TWO
Two-Week Entrée Plan A

*F*or God, who gives seed to
the farmer to plant, and later on,
good crops to harvest and eat,
will give you more and more
seed to plant and will make
it grow so that you can give
away more and more fruit
from your harvest.

2 Corinthians 9:10, TLB

Menu

· CALENDAR ·

Sunday	*Monday*	*Tuesday*	*Wednesday*	*Thursday*	*Friday*	*Saturday*
	Eat Out Cooking Day! 1	Chicken Packets 2	Mexican Stroganoff 3	French Bread Pizza 4	Calzones 5	Chili Verde 6
Spaghetti 7	Wild Rice Chicken 8	Balkan Meatballs 9	Marinated Flank Steak 10	Chicken Broccoli 11	Linguine à la Anne 12	Chili Hamburgers 13
Baked Eggs 14	Poulet de France 15	16	17	18	19	20
21	22	23	24	25	26	27
28	29	30				

GROCERY SHOPPING AND STAPLES LISTS

An asterisk (*) after an item indicates it can be stored until you cook the dish it will be served with. For example, the spaghetti noodles will not be cooked until the day you serve Spaghetti. Mark those items as a reminder that you will need them for an entrée.

When entrées require perishable foods to be refrigerated until served, you may want to use those dishes right away or buy the food the week you plan to prepare the dish. For example, fresh mushrooms would spoil by the end of a month.

For two-week entrée plan A, you will need these food items as well as the ones in the staples list that follows.

GROCERY SHOPPING LIST

Canned Goods

1 4-ounce can chopped, green chilies
2 10¾-ounce cans condensed cream of mushroom soup
1 10¾-ounce can condensed cream of chicken soup
1 12-ounce can evaporated skim milk
1 8-ounce and 2 4-ounce cans mushroom stems and pieces
1 11½-ounce jar salsa*
3 28-ounce cans Italian-style or plain crushed tomatoes in puree
1 12-ounce can tomato paste
1 8-ounce can sliced water chestnuts

Grains, Noodles, and Rice

4 hamburger buns
6 bread slices
1 loaf unsliced French bread (not sourdough)*
2 cups (approx.) seasoned croutons (1 cup croutons, ½ cup and ⅓ cup crushed crouton crumbs)
1 12-ounce package linguine
1 dozen corn tortillas*
1 8-ounce and 1 12-ounce package wide egg noodles*
8 ounces (1¼ cups) dry pinto beans
1 16-ounce package spaghetti*

1 12-ounce package seasoned bread stuffing—7-pound bird size (6 cups)

1 6¼-ounce package long grain and wild rice (Uncle Ben's Fast Cooking Long Grain and Wild Rice if available)

Frozen Foods

1 10-ounce package frozen, chopped broccoli

2 loaves frozen bread dough (Italian or French if available, otherwise wheat)

Dairy Products

9 eggs

¾ cup margarine

10 ounces (2½ cups) grated, mild cheddar cheese

10 ounces (2½ cups; 1 cup will be saved*) grated mozzarella cheese

4 ounces (1 cup) grated, low-fat Monterey Jack cheese*

4 ounces (1 cup) grated Parmesan cheese

2 ounces (½ cup) Romano cheese

1 3-ounce package cream cheese

1 8-ounce carton sour cream or low-fat yogurt*

2 8-ounce packages refrigerated crescent rolls*

7 cups milk

Meat and Poultry

10 pounds whole chicken or 8 pounds chicken breasts

1 pound boneless, skinless chicken breasts

1⅔ pounds cooked ham

2 pounds lean ground beef (or substitute ground turkey)

1 pound bulk Italian sausage

1⅓ pounds flank steak

½ of a 3-ounce package of sliced pepperoni*

2 pounds round steak

½ pound ground turkey

Produce

 1 small bunch celery
 8 cloves garlic
 1½ pounds brown or yellow onions
 1 bunch fresh parsley
 2 green bell peppers and 1 red bell pepper (or 3 green bell peppers)

STAPLES LIST

Make sure you have the following staples on hand; add those you don't have to the above shopping list:

 ground allspice
 dried basil leaves
 bay leaves (4)
 black pepper
 cayenne pepper
 chili powder (2 tablespoons)
 chili sauce (½ cup plus 1 tablespoon)
 chopped chives (¼ cup plus 1 tablespoon)
 ground cloves
 ground cumin
 curry powder
 all-purpose flour (¼ cup plus 1 tablespoon)
 ground ginger
 light mayonnaise (2 cups)
 minced onion
 nonstick spray
 ground nutmeg
 dried oregano leaves
 paprika
 red wine vinegar (about ¾ cup)
 salt
 seasoned salt
 soy sauce (¼ cup plus 1 teaspoon)

sugar
vegetable oil (1 cup)
waxed paper
Worcestershire sauce (2 teaspoons)

FREEZER CONTAINERS

The following list of freezer containers or flat baking dishes will be needed for the entrées in two-week cycle A. They're not the only containers in which you could freeze these foods, but the list gives you an idea of the size and number of containers you'll need.

10 sandwich bags:
Calzones

11 1-quart freezer bags:
Chicken Packets (2), French Bread Pizza (3), Poulet de France, Linguine à la Anne (2), Calzones (2), Chili Verde

6 1-gallon freezer bags:
Wild Rice Chicken, Calzones (2), Balkan Meatballs, Chili Hamburgers, Marinated Flank Steak

1 3-cup container:
French Bread Pizza

1 4-cup container:
Spaghetti Sauce

1 5-cup container:
Chili Verde

1 6-cup container:
Mexican Stroganoff

3 13x9x2-inch baking dishes:
Poulet de France, Baked Eggs, Linguine à la Anne

1 7x11x2-inch baking dish:
Chicken Broccoli

Heavy aluminum foil
French Bread Pizza

THE DAY BEFORE COOKING DAY

1. Freeze the 4 hamburger buns in a plastic bag and the French bread in heavy foil, with the package of pepperoni taped to the foil. Refrigerate crescent rolls.

2. Cut 1 pound of boneless, skinless chicken breasts into 1-inch cubes with kitchen scissors for Chili Verdes; refrigerate until needed.

3. In a large pot (may need two), place the 10 pounds of whole chickens (or 8 pounds of breasts) in about 3 quarts water, making sure they're completely covered. Heat to a boil; reduce heat. Cover and simmer until thickest pieces are done, about 45 minutes to 1 hour. Save and refrigerate 6⅓ cups chicken broth; discard remaining broth or use for soup.

   Cool chicken until ready to handle; remove skin and debone. Cut into bite-size pieces with kitchen scissors, which are easier to use than a knife. Refrigerate chicken pieces in two plastic bags.

4. Set out appliances, bowls, canned goods, dry ingredients, freezer containers, and recipes.

5. Thaw 2 loaves of frozen baking dough in the refrigerator overnight.

6. Rinse pinto beans; cover with water and soak overnight.

COOKING DAY ASSEMBLY ORDER

Make sure you've cleared the table and counters of unnecessary kitchenware to allow plenty of working room. It also helps to have fresh, damp washcloths and towels for wiping your hands and the cooking area. The day will go a lot smoother if you clean and organize as you work.

Before you prepare a recipe, gather all the spices and ingredients in the assembly area to save time and steps. When you finish the recipe, remove unneeded items and wipe off the work space.

Slightly undercook regular rice and noodles (al dente) that will be frozen. When you reheat them, they'll have a better consistency and won't turn mushy.

BEFORE ASSEMBLING DISHES

1. Cook and stir the bulk Italian sausage until brown in a large pot for Spaghetti Sauce. Take a minute after chopping the onions, garlic, and parsley to complete Spaghetti Sauce according to recipe. Start sauce boiling on the front burner, reduce heat, and then move pan to a back burner for 2 hours of simmering.

2. Perform all the chopping, grating, and slicing tasks.
   Onions: finely chop all (store in cold water in a container with a tight-fitting lid).
   Garlic: mince 8 cloves.
   Parsley: chop ½ cup.
   Celery: finely chop 1½ cups.
   Green and red bell peppers: chop ¼ cup plus 1 tablespoon green bell pepper; slice 1 green and 1 red pepper.
   Cheddar cheese: grate all.
   Monterey Jack cheese: grate all.
   Mozzarella cheese: grate 4 ounces; slice 6 ounces.
   Croutons: crush enough to make 1 cup crumbs.

3. Spray pans or baking dishes you will need with nonstick spray (check list of freezer containers on page 22).

4. As you assemble the chicken, ham, beef, and miscellaneous entrées, allow them to cool if necessary, put them in storage containers, and freeze them.

ASSEMBLE CHICKEN DISHES

1. Skim off and discard chicken fat from 6⅓ cups chicken broth.

2. Start the Chili Verde.

3. Cook rice for Wild Rice Chicken according to package directions.

4. Make filling for Chicken Packets in a medium bowl (mixing with hands works best), put mixture in a bag, and freeze.

5. Assemble Wild Rice Chicken.

6. Start Poulet de France.

7. Start cooking 10-ounce package of frozen, chopped broccoli.

8. Finish assembling Poulet de France.

9. Assemble Chicken Broccoli.

10. Add chicken and spices to Chili Verde, and simmer 10 more minutes.

11. Cool Spaghetti Sauce, and freeze as directed.

12. Freeze chicken dishes.

ASSEMBLE HAM DISHES

1. Dice 1⅔ pounds ham, placing 4 cups in one bowl and 1 cup in another.

2. Boil linguine according to package directions.

3. Assemble Baked Eggs.

4. Complete Linguine à la Anne.

5. Freeze ham dishes.

ASSEMBLE BEEF DISHES

1. Prepare Calzones and freeze.

2. Cut round steak in bite-size pieces.

3. Combine ingredients for Mexican Stroganoff, and start it simmering.

4. Assemble and broil Balkan Meatballs.

5. Prepare Marinated Flank Steak.

6. Prepare Chili Hamburger patties.

7. Freeze beef dishes.

COOKING DAY ASSEMBLY ORDER

RECIPES FOR TWO-WEEK ENTRÉE PLAN A

Each recipe offers complete instructions on how to prepare the dish. Food items with an asterisk (*) won't be prepared until you serve the entrée. For recipes calling for oven baking, preheat oven for about 10 minutes.

"Summary of processes" gives a quick overview of foods that need to be chopped, diced, grated, or sliced. "Freeze in" tells what bags and containers will be needed to freeze each entrée. "Serve with" offers suggestions of foods to accompany the meal. Some of the recipes for those foods are included in chapter 8; page numbers are indicated for easy reference. "Note" includes special instructions on how the entrée can be used in other ways.

SPAGHETTI SAUCE

1 pound bulk Italian sausage
1½ cups finely chopped onion
1 12-ounce can tomato paste
3 28-ounce cans Italian-style or plain crushed tomatoes in puree
2 cups water
4 teaspoons minced garlic (4 cloves)
4 bay leaves
2 tablespoons sugar
4 teaspoons dried basil leaves
2 teaspoons dried oregano leaves
4 tablespoons chopped fresh parsley
2 teaspoons salt
1 16-ounce package spaghetti*

*I*n a large pot, cook and stir the bulk Italian sausage with the onion until the meat is brown; drain fat. Add remaining ingredients, except the spaghetti. Bring sauce to a boil; reduce heat. Partly cover, and simmer for 2 hours, stirring occasionally. (If desired, simmer in a Crockpot instead of pot.) Makes 12 cups sauce.

After sauce has cooled, freeze 4 cups for Spaghetti and 3 cups for French Bread Pizza; divide remaining 5 cups sauce in half, and freeze in 2 1-quart bags for Calzones.

To prepare for serving Spaghetti, thaw sauce, and heat in a medium saucepan. Cook noodles according to package directions, drain, and pour sauce over them. Makes 6 servings.

Summary of processes: Chop 1½ cups onion, 4 tablespoons parsley; mince 4 cloves garlic

Freeze in: 4-cup container, Spaghetti; 3-cup container, French Bread Pizza; 2 1-quart freezer bags, Calzones

Serve with: Fresh Baked Asparagus (page 200), Cheesy-Herb Bread (page 180)

FRENCH BREAD PIZZA

1 loaf unsliced French bread (not sourdough)*
3 cups Spaghetti Sauce*
¼ cup grated Parmesan cheese*
1 cup grated mozzarella cheese*
3 ounces pepperoni slices (half a package)*

*T*his recipe is assembled on the day it's served. Put sauce in a 3-cup container, cheeses in 2 1-quart bags, and pepperoni in 1-quart bag; wrap bread in heavy foil. Freeze them together.

To prepare for serving, thaw French bread, sauce, grated cheeses, and pepperoni. Set oven to broil and/or 550°. Slice loaf of French bread in half lengthwise. Layer sauce, Parmesan cheese, pepperoni, and mozzarella cheese on each half. Place bread on baking sheet, and put in oven. Broil until mozzarella is melted. Cut pizza into serving-size pieces. Makes 6 to 8 servings.

Summary of processes: Grate 4 ounces mozzarella cheese

Freeze in: 3-cup container; 3 1-quart bags; foil for bread

Serve with: Waldorf salad

CHILI VERDE

8 ounces dry pinto beans (1¼ cups)
1 pound boneless, skinless chicken breasts
1 4-ounce can chopped green chilies
1 teaspoon ground cumin
¾ teaspoon dried oregano leaves
⅛ teaspoon ground cloves
⅛ teaspoon cayenne pepper
3 cups chicken broth
1 teaspoon minced garlic (1 clove)
1 teaspoon salt
⅔ cup finely chopped onion
1 cup grated low-fat Monterey Jack cheese*
1 dozen corn tortillas*
1 11½-ounce jar salsa*

*R*inse pinto beans, soak them in cold water overnight, then drain. Cut chicken into 1-inch cubes; cook until no longer pink in small amount of water. Combine chicken with chilies and seasonings; refrigerate until needed. At the same time, combine beans, chicken broth, garlic, salt, and onion in a large pot; bring to a boil. Reduce heat and simmer until beans are soft, about 1 hour. Add more water if necessary.

Combine chicken and spices with beans; simmer 10 more minutes. Cool and freeze. Grate cheese, put in a 1-quart bag, and attach it to the freezer container with the chili.

To serve, thaw chili and cheese. Simmer chili 30 minutes, stirring occasionally. Top chili with salsa and grated cheese; serve on warmed corn tortillas. Makes 5 servings.

Summary of processes: Soak ½ pound pinto beans overnight; cut 1 pound boneless chicken into cubes; finely chop ⅔ cup onion; grate 1 cup low-fat Monterey Jack cheese

Freeze in: 5-cup container; 1-quart bag

Serve with: Tossed green salad

WILD RICE CHICKEN

1 6¼-ounce package quick-cooking long grain and wild rice
1 cup cooked, chopped chicken
1 8-ounce can sliced water chestnuts, drained
1 cup finely chopped celery
1¼ cups finely chopped onion
1 cup light mayonnaise*
1 10¾-ounce can condensed cream of mushroom soup*

*C*ook rice according to package directions. Combine rice with chopped chicken, water chestnuts, celery, and onion; put mixture in a 1-gallon freezer bag.

To prepare for serving, thaw rice and chicken mixture, remove from bag, and place in a 2½-quart baking dish that has been sprayed with nonstick spray. Preheat oven to 325°. Stir mayonnaise and condensed cream of mushroom soup together, and spread over top of chicken. Cover and bake for 1 hour. Makes 6 servings.

Summary of processes: Chop 1 cup cooked chicken, 1 cup celery, and 1¼ cups onion

Freeze in: 1-gallon bag

Serve with: Cooked green beans, peach halves with cottage cheese topped with a maraschino cherry, and Blueberry Pie (page 192)

CHICKEN PACKETS

2 cups cooked, chopped chicken
1 3-ounce package cream cheese, softened
1 tablespoon chopped chives
2 tablespoons milk
Salt to taste
½ cup crushed, seasoned crouton crumbs*
2 8-ounce packages refrigerated crescent rolls*
¼ cup (½ stick) melted margarine*

*M*ix chicken, cream cheese, chives, milk, and salt in a medium bowl (mixing with hands works best) to make filling, and store in a 1-quart freezer bag. Put crouton crumbs in another 1-quart bag, attach it to bag of chicken filling, and freeze. Refrigerate crescent rolls.

To prepare for serving, thaw chicken mixture. Preheat oven to 350°. Unroll crescent rolls. Each tube will contain 4 rectangles of dough with a diagonal perforation. Press dough along each perforation so the rectangle halves will not separate. Place about ¼ cup of chicken mixture into the center of each rectangle. Fold dough over the filling, and pinch the edges to seal tightly. Dip each packet in melted margarine, and coat with crouton crumbs. Place packets on a baking sheet. Bake for 20 minutes or until golden brown. Packets are good either hot or cold. (Serve early in the month before date expires on crescent rolls.) Makes 8 packets.

Summary of processes: Chop 2 cups cooked chicken and 1 tablespoon chives

Freeze in: 2 1-quart bags

Serve with: Smoky Corn Chowder (page 198), baked apples stuffed with plump raisins

Note: These packets are a favorite with children.

RECIPES

POULET DE FRANCE

1 12-ounce package seasoned bread stuffing (6 cups)
2 tablespoons melted margarine
2 cups chicken broth, divided
3 cups chopped, cooked chicken
½ cup finely chopped onion
¼ cup minced chives
½ cup finely chopped celery
½ cup light mayonnaise
¾ teaspoon salt
2 eggs
1½ cups milk
1 10¾-ounce can condensed cream of mushroom soup
½ cup grated mild cheddar cheese

*I*n a medium bowl, mix stuffing, melted margarine, and 1¼ cups broth. Mix chicken, ¾ cup broth, onion, chives, celery, mayonnaise, and salt in another bowl.

Spread half the stuffing in a 13x9x2-inch baking dish treated with nonstick spray. Spread chicken mixture over stuffing. Cover with remaining stuffing. Whisk eggs, milk, and soup in a large bowl. Pour sauce evenly over stuffing. Cover dish with foil, and freeze. Put cheese in a small freezer bag, and attach it to dish.

To prepare for serving, thaw grated cheese and chicken dish. Preheat oven to 325°. Cover and bake for 30 minutes. Remove foil, sprinkle with cheese, and continue to bake, uncovered, for 10 minutes more. Makes 8 servings.

Summary of processes: Chop 3 cups cooked chicken, ½ cup onion, and ½ cup celery; mince ¼ cup chives; grate ½ cup mild cheddar cheese

Freeze in: 13x9x2-inch baking dish; 1-quart bag

Serve with: Cooked frozen peas, lemon gelatin with pears, Cranberry Tea (page 191)

Note: This is a super dish to take to a potluck dinner.

CHICKEN BROCCOLI

1 10-ounce package frozen, chopped broccoli
4 cups cooked, chopped chicken
1 10¾-ounce can condensed cream of chicken soup
½ cup light mayonnaise
1 4-ounce can mushroom stems and pieces, drained
¼ teaspoon curry powder
¾ cup grated Parmesan cheese, divided

*C*ook broccoli in boiling water according to package directions. Drain broccoli, and spread it in a 7x11x2-inch baking dish treated with nonstick spray. Mix chicken, soup, mayonnaise, mushrooms, curry powder, and ½ cup Parmesan cheese in a medium bowl. Spread chicken mixture over broccoli. Sprinkle ¼ cup Parmesan cheese over top. Cover dish with foil, and freeze.

To prepare for serving, thaw dish. Preheat oven to 350°. Cover and bake for 40 minutes. Remove foil, stir to bring colder food in center to the outside; bake 20 minutes more. Makes 6 servings.

Summary of processes: Chop 4 cups cooked chicken

Freeze in: 7x11x2-inch baking dish

Serve with: Croissants, Cranberry Cream Salad (page 196)

RECIPES

BAKED EGGS

6 bread slices, cut in cubes
2 cups grated mild cheddar cheese
1 cup cooked, cubed ham
¼ cup chopped green bell pepper
½ cup finely chopped onion
6 eggs
3 cups milk

*M*ix bread, cheese, ham, bell pepper, and onion; spread in a 13x9x2-inch baking dish treated with nonstick spray. Whisk eggs and milk together, and pour over top. Cover dish with foil and freeze.

To prepare for serving, thaw dish, and preheat oven to 375°. Bake, uncovered, for 45 minutes. Makes 8 to 10 servings.

Summary of processes: Cut bread and ham into cubes; grate 2 cups mild cheddar cheese; chop ¼ cup green bell pepper and ½ cup onion

Freeze in: 13x9x2-inch baking dish

Serve with: Hot Spiced Fruit (page 198)

Note: This dish is good with 6 slices cooked, crumbled bacon instead of ham. You can also make this dish the night before, refrigerate it, and serve it the next morning. It's nice for company brunch after church.

CHAPTER TWO

LINGUINE À LA ANNE

1 12-ounce package linguine
2 tablespoons margarine
2 tablespoons all-purpose flour
½ teaspoon salt
1 12-ounce can evaporated skim milk
1 4-ounce can mushroom stems and pieces, save liquid
1⅓ cups chicken broth
4 cups cooked, cubed ham
½ cup grated Romano cheese
1 sliced red bell pepper
1 sliced green bell pepper
1 tablespoon vegetable oil
1 cup seasoned croutons*

Cook linguine in a large pot according to package directions, drain, and return to pot. While linguine cooks, melt margarine in a medium saucepan over low heat. Stir in flour and salt, adding evaporated milk. Bring to a boil, stirring constantly. Boil and stir 1 minute. Add liquid from mushrooms and the chicken broth. Cook over medium heat, stirring constantly until bubbly and slightly thickened.

Add 2 cups sauce and drained mushrooms to linguine; toss until well mixed. Spoon linguine mixture into a 13x9x2-inch baking dish that has been treated with nonstick spray, pressing the linguine mixture up the sides to leave a slight hollow in center of dish.

Toss ham in remaining sauce; spread it in the center of the linguine. Sprinkle with Romano cheese, cover with foil, and freeze dish. Sauté red and green bell peppers in vegetable oil until soft; allow to cool. Put peppers in 1-quart freezer bag; attach this bag and croutons in a 1-quart freezer bag to the dish.

To prepare for serving, thaw dish, peppers, and croutons. Preheat oven to 400°. Bake dish, uncovered, for 20 minutes. Before serving, sprinkle croutons around edge of casserole. Reheat sautéed red and green bell peppers, and mound them in the center. Makes 8 servings.

Summary of processes: Cut ham into cubes; slice 1 red bell pepper and 1 green bell pepper

Freeze in: 13x9x2-inch baking dish; 2 1-quart bags

Serve with: Cooked zucchini, Orange Spiced Tea (page 191)

Note: Great for company that includes children.

RECIPES

CALZONES

2 loaves frozen bread dough (Italian, French, or white)
6 ounces grated mozzarella cheese
5 cups Spaghetti Sauce

*T*haw two loaves of bread dough. Divide each loaf into 5 parts. One at a time, roll each dough piece on a floured board or stretch with your hands, making 10 7-inch squares. Fold each dough square over a pinch of cheese to form a turnover, and pinch edges to seal.

Place each turnover in a small sandwich bag. Put 5 turnovers in a 1-gallon freezer bag. Divide sauce in half, and store in 2 1-quart freezer bags; enclose each bag of sauce in a bag of Calzones. Do the same with the remaining 5 turnovers.

To prepare for serving, thaw sauce; heat in a medium pan 10 to 15 minutes until bubbly. At the same time, take frozen turnovers out of bags, and place them about 2 inches apart on a baking sheet sprayed with nonstick spray. Preheat oven to 350°. Bake for about 20 minutes. Turnovers will be golden brown when done. Ladle sauce on top of turnovers and serve. Makes 10 servings.

Freeze in: 2 1-gallon bags; 2 1-quart bags; 10 sandwich bags

Serve with: Tossed salad with Italian dressing

Note: All ages love these! They're convenient, since you can bake only as many as are needed at a time. Reheat for lunches.

CHAPTER TWO

MEXICAN STROGANOFF

2 pounds round steak
1 cup finely chopped onion
2 teaspoons minced garlic (2 cloves)
2 tablespoons vegetable oil
⅓ cup red wine vinegar
1¾ cups water
½ cup chili sauce
1 tablespoon paprika
1 tablespoon chili powder
2 teaspoons seasoned salt
1 teaspoon soy sauce
1 8-ounce can mushroom stems and pieces, drained
1 12-ounce package wide egg noodles*
1 8-ounce carton sour cream or low-fat yogurt*
3 tablespoons all-purpose flour*

*C*ut steak into bite-size pieces. Cook and stir steak, onion, and garlic in oil in a large saucepan over medium heat until brown. Drain off oil. Stir vinegar, water, chili sauce, paprika, chili powder, seasoned salt, soy sauce, and mushrooms into steak mixture. Bring to a boil; reduce heat. Cover and simmer 1 hour until meat is tender. Cool and store in freezer container.

To prepare for serving, thaw meat mixture and heat in saucepan until bubbly. Cook egg noodles according to package directions. Stir sour cream or low-fat yogurt and flour together; combine with stroganoff. Heat to a boil, stirring constantly. Reduce heat, simmer, and stir about 1 minute. Serve stroganoff over noodles. Makes 6 to 8 servings.

Summary of processes: Cut steak in bite-size pieces; chop 1 cup onion; mince 2 cloves garlic

Freeze in: 6-cup container

Serve with: Tomatoes stuffed with guacamole, corn on the cob

RECIPES

BALKAN MEATBALLS

1 egg
¼ cup milk
⅓ cup crushed seasoned croutons
¾ teaspoon salt
¾ teaspoon sugar
¼ teaspoon ground ginger
¼ teaspoon ground nutmeg
¼ teaspoon ground allspice
1 pound lean ground beef
½ pound ground turkey
1 tablespoon minced onion
1 8-ounce package wide egg noodles*
2 tablespoons margarine*
¼ cup all-purpose flour*
2 cups milk*
Parsley for garnish*

*I*n a medium mixing bowl, beat egg with milk. Mix in the crushed croutons, salt, sugar, and spices. Add beef, turkey, and onion; mix thoroughly. Preheat oven to broil and/or 550°. Shape meat mixture into meatballs the size of walnuts. Place meatballs on a rimmed cookie sheet; broil until lightly browned. Cool; put meatballs in a large bag and freeze them.

To prepare for serving, thaw meatballs. Cook noodles according to package directions. At the same time, make white sauce in a large skillet. Melt margarine over low heat. Add flour, stirring constantly until mixture is smooth and bubbly. Gradually stir in milk. Heat to boiling over medium heat, stirring constantly. Boil and stir 1 minute until thick and smooth. Add meatballs to sauce. Bring to a boil; reduce heat. Cover pan; simmer 15 minutes, stirring occasionally. Serve meatballs and sauce over wide egg noodles. Chop parsley; sprinkle over top. Makes 4 servings.

Summary of processes: Chop ⅔ cup onion

Freeze in: 1-gallon bag

Serve with: Cooked, fresh broccoli

MARINATED FLANK STEAK

½ cup vegetable oil
¼ cup soy sauce
¼ cup red wine vinegar
2 teaspoons Worcestershire sauce
½ teaspoon ground ginger
1 teaspoon minced garlic (1 clove)
1⅓ pounds flank steak

*M*ix first six ingredients for marinade. Put flank steak in a freezer bag, pour marinade over it, seal bag, and freeze.

To prepare for serving, thaw flank steak, remove from marinade, and barbecue 8 to 10 minutes per side; or set oven control to broil and/or 550°. Broil steak 6 inches from heat until brown, turning once, about 6 minutes on one side and 4 minutes on the other. Cut steak across grain at slanted angle into thin slices. Makes 4 servings.

Summary of processes: Mince 1 clove garlic

Freeze in: 1-gallon bag

Serve with: Twice-Baked Potatoes Deluxe (page 200), cooked zucchini

RECIPES

CHILI HAMBURGERS

1 pound lean ground beef or turkey
2 tablespoons finely chopped green bell pepper
1 tablespoon minced onion
1 tablespoon chili powder
1 tablespoon chili sauce
¼ teaspoon black pepper
½ teaspoon salt
4 hamburger buns*

*T*horoughly mix all ingredients except hamburger buns. Shape into 4 hamburger patties. Freeze in a large freezer bag, with waxed paper between each one.

To prepare for serving, thaw patties and hamburger buns. Grill or fry patties to desired pinkness in center. Serve on warmed hamburger buns. Makes 4 servings.

Summary of processes: Chop 2 tablespoons green bell pepper

Freeze in: 1-gallon bag

Serve with: French fries or baked beans, Jiffy Salad (page 196)

CHAPTER THREE
A Low-Fat Two-Week Entrée Plan

*H*e makes grass grow for
the cattle, and plants for man
to cultivate—bringing forth
food from the earth.

Psalm 104:14

Menu

· C A L E N D A R ·

Sunday	Monday	Tuesday	Wednesday	Thursday	Friday	Saturday
	Eat Out Cooking Day! 1	Hearty Hamburger Tomato Stew 2	Chinese Chicken Morsels 3	Veggie Pizza 4	Grilled Fish 5	Chicken Spaghetti 6
Mandarin Orange Chicken 7	Vegetable Lasagna 8	Stove-Top Barbecued Chicken 9	Split Pea Soup 10	Blackened Chicken Breast 11	Chicken Cacciatore 12	Pizza Roll-Ups 13
Savory Beef 14	Chili Verde 15	16	17	18	19	20
21	22	23	24	25	26	27
28	29	30				

CHAPTER THREE

GROCERY SHOPPING AND STAPLES LISTS

An asterisk (*) after an item indicates that it should be stored until you cook the dish it will be served with. For example, the corn tortillas and salsa will not be used until the day you serve Chili Verde. Mark those items as a reminder that you will need them for an entrée.

When entrées require perishable foods to be refrigerated until served, you may want to prepare those dishes right away or buy the food the week you plan to make the dish. For example, fresh mushrooms would spoil by the end of a month.

For the low-fat entrée plan, you will need these food items as well as the ones in the staples list that follows.

GROCERY SHOPPING LIST

Canned Goods

1 16-ounce can corn

1 4-ounce can chopped green chilies

1 16-ounce can cut green beans

1 8-ounce bottle lemon juice (½ cup)

1 11-ounce can mandarin orange sections*

1 8-ounce can mushroom stems and pieces

1 2-ounce jar pimientos

1 11½-ounce jar salsa*

1 46-ounce can tomato juice

1 6-ounce can tomato paste

5 28-ounce cans Italian-style or plain crushed tomatoes in puree

1 3-ounce can sliced ripe olives

Grains, Noodles, Rice, and Seasonings

1 8-ounce package lasagna

1 8-ounce package dry pinto beans

1 16-ounce package regular rice (1 cup*)

6 sandwich rolls*

1 12-ounce package spaghetti

1 1½ package dry spaghetti sauce seasoning mix

1 8-ounce package wide egg noodles

1 16-ounce package spinach or wide egg noodles

1 12-ounce package dry, green split peas

1 dozen corn tortillas*

Frozen Foods

1¼ pounds frozen fish fillets (halibut, swordfish, or orange roughy)*

2 loaves frozen French, Italian, or all-purpose bread dough or Dawn's French
 Bread (page 183)

1 6-ounce can frozen orange juice concentrate

Dairy Products

8 ounces low-fat cheddar cheese

4 ounces low-fat Monterey Jack cheese

15 ounces part-skim mozzarella cheese

16 ounces low-fat ricotta cheese

Meat and Poultry

2 pounds skinned chicken pieces

7 pounds boneless, skinless chicken breasts

2 pounds lean ground beef or turkey

2 pounds beef round tip steak

½ pound cooked turkey ham

Produce

3 green bell peppers

1 small red bell pepper (opt.)

2 medium stems fresh broccoli

5 carrots (2¾ cups sliced)

1 bunch celery

4 cloves garlic

1¾ pounds fresh mushrooms (8 cups sliced)

1 bunch green onions

3 pounds brown or yellow onions (6 medium)

1 bunch fresh parsley

5 or 6 new potatoes

1 medium zucchini

STAPLES LIST

Make sure you have the following staples on hand; add those you don't have to the above shopping list:

dried basil leaves

bay leaf

beef bouillon cubes (2)

brown sugar

catsup (⅓ cup)

celery seed

chicken bouillon cubes (6)

chili powder

ground cloves

ground cumin

Dijon mustard (¼ cup)

dill weed

dry mustard

all-purpose flour

garlic powder

garlic salt

ground ginger

Italian herb seasoning

light mayonnaise

low-fat margarine

nonstick spray

olive oil

onion powder

dried oregano leaves

paprika

Parmesan cheese

pepper: cayenne, white, freshly ground black, and regular black

salt

soy sauce (¾ cup)

sugar

dried thyme leaves

vegetable oil (about ½ cup)

white vinegar

Worcestershire sauce (about 3 tablespoons)

FREEZER CONTAINERS

The following list of freezer containers or flat baking dishes will be needed for the entrées in the two-week cycle. They're not the only containers in which you could freeze these foods, but the list gives you an idea of the size and number of containers you'll need.

1 empty spice jar or small container:
Blackened Chicken

5 1-gallon freezer bags:
Pizza Roll-Ups (4), Chinese Chicken Morsels

8 1-quart freezer bags:
Pizza Roll-Ups (4), Grilled Fish, Blackened Chicken, Chicken Spaghetti, Chili Verde

Heavy aluminum foil:
Veggie Pizza, Vegetable Lasagna

1 12-inch pizza pan or 10-inch pie plate:
Veggie Pizza

2 4-cup freezer containers:
Stove-Top Barbecued Chicken, Mandarin Orange Chicken

1 5-cup freezer container:
Chili Verde

1 6-cup freezer container:
Split Pea Soup

2 8-cup freezer containers:
Savory Beef, Chicken Cacciatore

2 16-cup freezer containers:
Hearty Hamburger Tomato Stew, Chicken Spaghetti

1 13x9x2-inch baking dish:
Vegetable Lasagna

THE DAY BEFORE COOKING DAY

1. Freeze fish fillets, sandwich rolls, and 1½-pounds boneless, skinless chicken breasts for Blackened Chicken Breasts.

2. Use kitchen scissors or knife to cut 2 pounds raw, boneless chicken breasts into 1-inch cubes for Mandarin Orange Chicken and Chinese Chicken Morsels; refrigerate until needed.

3. In a large skillet, sauté remaining 3½-pounds boneless, skinless chicken breasts in a small amount of water until no longer pink in the center. Use kitchen scissors or knife to cut cooled chicken into 1-inch cubes. Store chicken in the refrigerator.

4. Set out appliances, bowls, canned goods, dry ingredients, freezer containers, and recipes.

5. Thaw 2 loaves of frozen bread dough in refrigerator overnight.

6. Rinse green split peas, and soak them covered with cold water overnight. Do the same for pinto beans.

COOKING DAY ASSEMBLY ORDER

Make sure you've cleared the table and counters of unnecessary kitchenware to allow plenty of working room. It also helps to have fresh, damp washcloths and towels for wiping your hands and the cooking area. The day will go smoother if you clean and organize as you work.

Before you prepare a recipe, gather all the spices and ingredients in the assembly area to save time and steps. When you finish the recipe, remove unneeded items, and wipe off the work space.

Slightly undercook regular rice and noodles (al dente) that will be frozen. When you reheat them, they will have a better consistency and won't turn mushy.

BEFORE ASSEMBLING DISHES

1. Put out 6-ounce can of frozen orange juice concentrate to thaw.

2. Brown 2 pounds of ground beef or turkey, drain, and blot on a paper towel.

3. Perform all chopping, grating, and slicing tasks.

      Turkey ham: cut into cubes.

      Beef: slice round tip steak into strips about 2 inches long.

      Onions: slice 2 onions; chop the rest.

      Green onions: chop onion bulbs only; discard green tops.

      Broccoli: chop fine tops of 2 medium stems including small amount of stems.

      Carrots: slice 2¾ cups.

      Celery: chop 1⅓ cups and slice 3 stalks, storing them in separate small bags.

      Garlic: mince 4 cloves.

      Mushrooms: slice all (8 cups).

      Parsley: chop the whole bunch, discarding most of stems.

      Green bell peppers: chop 2, slice 1.

      Red bell pepper: chop ½ cup.

      Zucchini: chop 1 cup.

      Mozzarella, cheddar, and Monterey Jack cheeses: grate all; put in separate bags.

4. Treat baking dishes and pie or pizza pans you will need with nonstick spray (check list of freezer containers on page 46).

5. As you assemble each group of the following entrées, allow them to cool if necessary, put them in storage containers and freeze.

ASSEMBLE GROUP 1 ENTRÉES

1. Combine ingredients for Italian Tomato Sauce and start it simmering.

2. Assemble and bake Veggie Pizza.

3. Roll out dough for Pizza Roll-Ups. Assemble and bake them.

4. Mix ingredients for Hearty Hamburger Tomato Stew and start it simmering.

5. As soon as the above dishes are completed and have cooled, label each one and freeze.

ASSEMBLE GROUP 2 ENTRÉES

1. Cook lasagna and broccoli for Vegetable Lasagna, and then finish assembling it.

2. Make marinade for Grilled Fish.

3. Label and freeze these dishes.

ASSEMBLE GROUP 3 ENTRÉES

1. Assemble and start cooking Split Pea Soup and Chili Verde.

2. Complete Savory Beef in a skillet. Allow to cool, label and freeze.

ASSEMBLE GROUP 4 ENTRÉES

1. Make Stove-Top Barbecued Chicken in one large skillet or pan with lid and Chicken Cacciatore in another.

2. While these are simmering, assemble Chinese Chicken Morsels.

3. Mix spices for Blackened Chicken Breasts.

4. Prepare Mandarin Orange Chicken.

5. Assemble Chicken Spaghetti, cooking noodles while chicken and tomato sauce are simmering.

6. Complete Split Pea Soup and Chili Verde; allow to cool.

7. Label and freeze this last batch of dishes.

Take a minute to enjoy looking into your freezer at all the food you've prepared!

RECIPES FOR THE LOW-FAT ENTRÉE PLAN

Each recipe offers complete instructions on how to prepare the dish. Food items with an asterisk (*) won't be prepared until you serve the entrée. For recipes calling for oven baking, preheat oven for about 10 minutes.

"Summary of processes" gives a quick overview of foods that need to be chopped, diced, grated, or sliced. "Freeze in" tells what bags and containers will be needed to freeze each entrée. "Serve with" offers suggestions of foods to accompany the meal. Some of the recipes for those foods are included in chapter 8; page numbers are indicated for easy reference. "Note" includes special instructions on how the entrée can be used in other ways.

ITALIAN TOMATO SAUCE

3 28-ounce cans Italian-style or plain crushed tomatoes in puree
3 tablespoons sugar
3 tablespoons Italian herb seasoning
6 tablespoons chopped, fresh parsley
3 tablespoons dried basil leaves
3 teaspoons garlic salt
1½ teaspoons pepper

Mix all the ingredients in a heavy, large pot. Bring to a boil; reduce heat. Simmer 15 minutes, stirring occasionally. Save 3½ cups sauce for Vegetable Lasagna and 2 cups for Veggie Pizza. Divide remaining sauce into four 1-cup portions, and put in four 1-quart bags for Pizza Roll-Ups. Makes 9½ cups.

Summary of Processes: Chop 6 tablespoons parsley

Freeze in: 4 1-quart bags

VEGGIE PIZZA

¼ cup chopped onion
¼ cup chopped red bell pepper (opt.)
¼ cup chopped green bell pepper
1 cup chopped zucchini
1 cup sliced fresh mushrooms
1 tablespoon vegetable oil
½ cup grated part-skim mozzarella cheese
1 loaf frozen French, Italian or all-purpose bread dough, or Dawn's
     French Bread (page 183)
2 cups Italian Tomato Sauce

*P*reheat oven to 400°. Sauté vegetables in oil, drain well, and allow to cool. Stir in cheese. Roll dough into a ½-inch-thick circle. Put dough on a 12-inch pizza pan or 10-inch pie plate. Spread Italian Tomato Sauce on pizza. Spoon vegetable mixture over sauce. Bake pizza for 20 minutes. Cool, cover pizza with heavy aluminum foil, and freeze.

To prepare for serving, thaw and then heat pizza in a preheated 400° oven for about 20 minutes. Makes 6 servings.

Summary of processes: Chop ¼ cup onion, ¼ cup red bell pepper, ¼ cup green bell pepper, 1 cup zucchini; slice 1 cup fresh mushrooms; grate ½ cup part-skim mozzarella cheese

Freeze in: 12-inch pizza pan or 10-inch pie pan; heavy aluminum foil

Serve with: Lemon gelatin with pears

Note: A tasty addition to this pizza is ½ pound browned turkey sausage, 1 teaspoon parsley, 1 teaspoon dried basil leaves, 1 teaspoon dried oregano leaves, and ½ teaspoon salt.

PIZZA ROLL-UPS

1 loaf frozen French, Italian, or all-purpose bread dough, or Dawn's
    French Bread (page 183)
1 pound lean ground beef or turkey (2½ cups browned)
1 teaspoon salt
½ teaspoon pepper
2 cups grated part-skim mozzarella cheese
1 teaspoon Italian herb seasoning
1 tablespoon chopped fresh parsley
4 cups Italian Tomato Sauce*

*T*haw dough; roll it into a 14x24-inch rectangle about ¼-inch thick. Brown ground beef or turkey; stir in remaining ingredients except Italian Tomato Sauce. Spoon filling evenly onto dough, slightly pressing filling into dough.

Roll dough lengthwise like a jelly roll, and cut into 24 1-inch slices. Treat 2 rimmed cookie sheets with nonstick spray; lay slices on sheets about an inch apart. Preheat oven to 400°. Let roll-ups sit for 10 minutes. Bake for 20 to 25 minutes or till golden brown. Cool roll-ups, and freeze in 4 1-gallon bags, 6 per bag. Slip a 1-quart bag with 1 cup sauce into each bag of Pizza Roll-Ups.

To prepare, thaw roll-ups and warm them in a preheated 400° oven for 10 minutes. Or put them frozen in the microwave; heat on high for about 2 minutes. Serve with warmed Italian Tomato Sauce. Makes 24 servings.

Summary of processes: Chop 1 tablespoon parsley; grate 2 cups part-skim mozzarella cheese

Freeze in: 4 1-gallon bags, Roll-Ups; 4 1-quart bags, Italian Tomato Sauce

Serve with: Tossed green salad

Note: These roll-ups are super for picnics or nights when the family must eat in shifts. They can be eaten warm or cold. They're also a favorite with kids and an easy snack.

RECIPES

HEARTY HAMBURGER TOMATO STEW

1 pound lean ground beef or turkey (2½ cups browned)
1¼ cups chopped onion
2 cups peeled and sliced carrots
1 cup chopped green bell pepper
1 cup sliced fresh mushrooms
1 16-ounce can cut green beans, drained
1 16-ounce can corn, drained
3 stalks sliced celery
1 46-ounce can tomato juice
2 teaspoons sugar
1 teaspoon celery seed
Salt and pepper to taste

*B*rown ground beef or turkey in a large saucepan. Mix in remaining ingredients; bring to a boil; reduce heat. Simmer, covered, 30 minutes, stirring occasionally. Cool and freeze.

To prepare for serving, thaw stew. Then bring to a boil; reduce heat; simmer 10 minutes. Makes 8 servings.

Summary of processes: Chop 1¼ cups onion and 1 cup green bell pepper; peel and slice 2 cups carrots, 1 cup fresh mushrooms, and 3 stalks celery

Freeze in: 16-cup container

Serve with: Cornbread or wheat crackers

VEGETABLE LASAGNA

1 8-ounce package lasagna
2 medium stems finely chopped broccoli florets
1 16-ounce carton low-fat ricotta cheese
1 cup grated part-skim mozzarella cheese
1 8-ounce can mushroom stems and pieces, drained
2 chopped green onion bulbs (without greens)
2 teaspoons dried basil leaves
1½ teaspoons crumbled dried oregano leaves
¼ cup finely chopped fresh parsley
Dash of fresh ground black pepper
3½ cups Italian Tomato Sauce

*B*oil lasagna 10 minutes or until al dente, stirring occasionally to prevent noodles from sticking. Drain noodles, rinse in cold water, and then lay them next to each other on waxed paper to dry. Cook broccoli 5 minutes in boiling water.

Combine cheeses, vegetables, herbs, and pepper in a medium bowl. In a 13x9x2-inch dish that has been treated with nonstick spray, layer lasagna noodles and spread with half the cheese mixture and half the tomato sauce. Repeat process, topping with noodles and covering with sauce. Wrap dish with foil and freeze.

To prepare for serving, thaw dish. Preheat oven to 350°. Cover and bake for 20 minutes. Remove foil, and bake 15 to 20 minutes more until heated through. Makes 12 servings.

Summary of processes: Grate 1 cup part-skim mozzarella cheese; chop 2 medium broccoli stems, 2 green onion bulbs, ¼ cup parsley

Freeze in: 13x9x2-inch baking dish

Serve with: Fresh fruit salad, bread sticks

Note: For an alternate way to prepare this entrée, use large shell pasta. Cook pasta as directed on package until al dente. Stuff each shell with cheese mixture. Freeze stuffed shells on a rimmed baking sheet. When they're hard, transfer them to a freezer bag. Freeze sauce in a separate bag taped to pasta bag. Thaw number of shells and amount of sauce desired. Warm them in a preheated 350° oven about 20 minutes. Serve shells with warmed sauce poured over them.

RECIPES

GRILLED FISH

1¼ pounds frozen fish fillets (halibut, swordfish, or orange roughy)*
5 or 6 new potatoes*
½ cup soy sauce
¼ cup water
¼ chicken bouillon cube
2 tablespoons olive oil
1 tablespoon brown sugar
2 teaspoons minced garlic (2 cloves)
½ teaspoon ground ginger

*F*reeze fish fillets, and store new potatoes until you're ready to serve them. Whisk remaining ingredients in a small bowl to make marinade. Freeze in a plastic bag taped to fish fillet package.

To prepare for serving, thaw marinade and fish fillets. Marinate fish in refrigerator 30 minutes. Prepare new potatoes. Heat 1 cup salted water to a boil; add potatoes. Cover, heat till boiling; then reduce heat. Simmer, tightly covered, until tender, 30 to 35 minutes; drain.

At the same time, remove fish from marinade. Preheat oven to broil and/or 550°. Broil or grill fish for 10 minutes per inch of thickness or until fish flakes easily with a fork. Baste frequently with marinade while cooking. If fish is more than 1-inch thick, turn once during cooking. Makes 4 servings.

Summary of processes: Mince 2 garlic cloves

Freeze in: 1-quart bag taped to fish fillet package

Serve with: Tossed green salad

Split Pea Soup

1 12-ounce package dry, green split peas
3 cups water
½ pound cooked, cubed turkey ham
¾ teaspoon onion powder
⅛ teaspoon dried thyme leaves
⅛ teaspoon freshly ground pepper
⅓ cup chopped celery
¾ cup peeled and sliced carrots
1 cup chopped onion
1 bay leaf
Salt to taste

*R*inse split peas, soak them in cold water overnight; drain. Put peas with remaining ingredients in a large saucepan. Bring to a boil; reduce heat. Stirring occasionally, simmer about 2 hours until peas are tender and turn pasty. Cool and freeze.

To serve, thaw peas and simmer until warmed through. If peas are too condensed, add water to make consistency of thick soup. Makes 6 servings.

Summary of processes: Soak split peas in water overnight; cut ham into cubes; peel and slice ¾ cup carrots; chop 1 cup onion, ⅓ cup celery

Freeze in: 6-cup container

Serve with: Orange slices or canned peaches, cornbread

RECIPES

CHILI VERDE

1 8-ounce package dry pinto beans (1¼ cups)
1 pound boneless, skinless chicken breasts
1 4-ounce can chopped green chilies
1 teaspoon ground cumin
¾ teaspoon dried oregano leaves
⅛ teaspoon ground cloves
⅛ teaspoon cayenne pepper
3 cups water
3 chicken bouillon cubes
1 teaspoon minced garlic (1 clove)
1 teaspoon salt
⅔ cup finely chopped onion
1 cup grated low-fat Monterey Jack cheese*
1 11½-ounce jar salsa*
1 dozen corn tortillas*

*R*inse pinto beans, soak them in cold water overnight, then drain. Cut chicken into 1-inch cubes; cook until no longer pink in small amount of water or vegetable oil. Combine chicken with chilies and seasonings; refrigerate until needed. At the same time, combine beans, water, bouillon cubes, garlic, salt, and onion in a large pot; bring to a boil.

Reduce heat and simmer until beans are soft, about 1 hour. Add more water if necessary.

Combine chicken and spices with beans; simmer 10 minutes more. Cool and freeze. Grate cheese, put it in a 1-quart bag, and attach it to the freezer container with the chili.

To serve, thaw chili and cheese. Simmer chili 30 minutes, stirring occasionally. Top chili with salsa and grated cheese; serve on warmed corn tortillas. Makes 5 servings.

Summary of processes: Soak ½ pound pinto beans overnight; cut 1 pound boneless chicken into cubes; finely chop ⅔ cup onion; grate 1 cup low-fat Monterey Jack cheese

Freeze in: 5-cup container; 1-quart bag

Serve with: Tossed green salad

SAVORY BEEF

2 pounds beef round tip steak
Freshly ground black pepper to taste
1 cup sliced fresh mushrooms
1 sliced onion
3 tablespoons vegetable oil
3 tablespoons all-purpose flour
2 cups water
2 beef bouillon cubes
2 tablespoons tomato paste
1 teaspoon dry mustard
¼ teaspoon dried oregano leaves
¼ teaspoon dill weed
2 tablespoons Worcestershire sauce
1 8-ounce package wide egg noodles*

Cut beef into thin strips about 2 inches long. Sprinkle beef with pepper, and set meat aside in a cool place. In a heavy skillet, sauté mushrooms and onion in oil until golden; remove them from skillet. Put meat in same skillet; cook and stir steak quickly on all sides until it's brown but still rare in the center. Remove meat, and set aside.

Blend flour into the drippings in skillet, gradually adding water and beef bouillon. Bring to a boil. Stir constantly until smooth and slightly thick. Mix in tomato paste, dry mustard, oregano, dill weed, and Worcestershire sauce. Stir meat, mushrooms, and onion into sauce. Cool meat mixture and freeze.

To prepare for serving, thaw beef. Prepare noodles according to package directions. Heat beef in a saucepan over medium heat, stirring constantly until bubbly. Serve meat over noodles. Makes 6 servings.

Summary of processes: Slice 1 cup fresh mushrooms and 1 onion

Freeze in: 8-cup container

Serve with: French-cut green beans

Note: Use any leftover beef for sandwiches.

STOVE-TOP BARBECUED CHICKEN

1 teaspoon vegetable oil
1 cup finely chopped onion
⅓ cup catsup
⅓ cup water
4 teaspoons white vinegar
4 teaspoons brown sugar
1½ teaspoons Worcestershire sauce
½ teaspoon chili powder
¼ teaspoon crushed celery seed
2 pounds skinned chicken pieces
1 16-ounce package spinach or wide egg noodles (use half)*

*H*eat oil in a large, nonstick skillet; sauté onion until tender. Stir in catsup, water, vinegar, brown sugar, Worcestershire sauce, chili powder, and celery seed. Bring sauce to a boil. Add the chicken to the skillet, placing the side down that has the skin removed; spoon sauce over the pieces. Bring to a boil; reduce heat. Cover and simmer 30 minutes. Turn chicken pieces, and simmer, covered, for about 20 minutes more or until chicken is cooked through. Cool and freeze chicken and sauce.

To prepare for serving, thaw chicken and sauce; put in a large skillet and cook over medium heat, stirring constantly until bubbly. Cook half package of spinach or egg noodles according to directions; serve chicken over noodles. Makes 4 servings.

Summary of processes: Chop 1 cup onion

Freeze in: 4-cup container

Serve with: Corn on the cob, Low-Calorie Chocolate Cake (page 194)

CHICKEN CACCIATORE

1 pound boneless, skinless chicken breasts (2 cups cooked)
1 tablespoon vegetable oil
1 sliced medium onion
½ sliced green bell pepper
2 cups sliced fresh mushrooms
1 teaspoon minced garlic (1 clove)
1 28-ounce can Italian-style or plain crushed tomatoes in puree
2 tablespoons chopped fresh parsley
1 teaspoon salt
¼ teaspoon pepper
2 teaspoons Italian herb seasoning
1 teaspoon dried basil leaves
Parmesan cheese*
1 16-ounce package spinach or wide egg noodles (use half)*

*C*ut chicken into 1-inch cubes. In a large skillet, sauté chicken in vegetable oil until no longer pink in the center. Remove chicken from skillet and sauté onion, green bell pepper, mushrooms, and garlic until onion is transparent. Add chicken and remaining ingredients except Parmesan cheese and noodles to the skillet. Simmer 15 minutes. Allow sauce to cool, put in an 8-cup container or dish, and freeze.

To serve, thaw dish and preheat oven to 350°. Bake chicken in a 13x9x2-inch baking dish for 35 minutes. Cook half package spinach or egg noodles according to directions. Serve chicken over noodles, and sprinkle on Parmesan cheese. Makes 6 servings.

Summary of processes: Cut 1 pound chicken into cubes; slice 1 medium onion, ½ green bell pepper, 2 cups fresh mushrooms; mince 1 clove garlic

Freeze in: 8-cup container or dish

Serve with: Cooked baby carrots, Dawn's French Bread (page 183)

RECIPES

CHINESE CHICKEN MORSELS

1 pound boneless, skinless chicken breasts (2 cups)
½ cup lemon juice
¼ cup soy sauce
¼ cup Dijon mustard
2 teaspoons vegetable oil
¼ teaspoon cayenne pepper
1 cup regular, uncooked rice*

*C*ut chicken breasts (kitchen scissors work best) into 1-inch cubes. Mix lemon juice, soy sauce, mustard, oil, and pepper. Put marinade and chicken cubes in a 1-gallon bag and store in the freezer.

To prepare for serving, thaw chicken and remove from marinade. Warm marinade in a small saucepan. Place cubes about an inch apart on broiler pan treated with nonstick spray. Broil 4 to 5 inches from heat for 7 minutes, brushing with marinade once. Turn chicken cubes and broil another 4 minutes. Meanwhile, prepare rice according to package directions. Heat remaining marinade and serve over rice. Makes 4 to 5 servings.

Summary of processes: Cut chicken into 1-inch cubes

Freeze in: 1-gallon bag

Serve with: Sliced, fresh tomatoes or tossed salad, Spicy Pumpkin Muffins (page 188)

Note: For a luncheon alternative, toss sautéed or broiled chicken morsels with mixed salad greens, shredded carrots, cherry tomatoes, chopped green bell pepper, sliced water chestnuts, and croutons. Use your favorite low-calorie dressing.

BLACKENED CHICKEN BREASTS

1½ pounds boneless, skinless chicken breasts*
6 sandwich rolls*
Spice Mix*
    2 teaspoons paprika
    1 teaspoon onion powder
    1 teaspoon garlic powder
    ¼ teaspoon cayenne pepper
    ½ teaspoon white pepper
    ½ teaspoon black pepper
    ½ teaspoon salt
    ½ teaspoon dried thyme leaves
    ½ teaspoon dried oregano leaves
¼ cup (½ stick) melted low-fat margarine or light mayonnaise*
2 tablespoons vegetable oil*
Low-fat margarine or light mayonnaise*

*F*reeze chicken and sandwich rolls until ready to serve. Mix spices; store in a covered container such as an empty spice jar, which you've labeled "Blackened Chicken Spices."

To serve, thaw rolls and chicken. Coat each piece of chicken with about 1 tablespoon spice mix. The mixture is hot and spicy, so adjust amount for taste of each person. Using a pastry brush, baste each piece of chicken with melted, low-fat margarine or light mayonnaise. Grill chicken, basting with low-fat margarine or mayonnaise after turning once. Grill about 10 minutes or until no longer pink in the middle. Or cook chicken in a large, nonstick skillet in hot oil over medium heat. Cook, turning chicken once, until it's done, about 10 minutes. Serve on sandwich rolls spread with a little margarine or light mayonnaise. Makes 6 servings.

Summary of processes: Mix spices

Freeze in: 1-quart bag

Serve with: Applesauce, carrot and celery strips

Note: Use spice mix on your favorite fish fillets.

MANDARIN ORANGE CHICKEN

1 pound boneless, skinless chicken breasts (2 cups)
1 tablespoon vegetable oil
2 cups sliced, fresh mushrooms
2 teaspoons all-purpose flour
⅔ cup water
1 6-ounce can frozen orange juice concentrate, thawed
½ cup thinly sliced green onion bulbs (without greens)
2 chicken bouillon cubes
1 cup regular, uncooked rice*
1 11-ounce can mandarin orange sections, drained*

*C*ut chicken into 1-inch chunks with kitchen scissors or knife. Heat oil in large skillet; add chicken, and cook on medium high until browned on both sides. Remove and set chicken aside. In the same skillet, cook mushrooms over medium high, stirring constantly. Sprinkle flour over mushrooms, stirring quickly to combine. Gradually stir in water, orange juice concentrate, green onions, and bouillon cubes. Stirring constantly, bring to a boil. Reduce heat, add chicken, and let simmer 3 to 4 minutes. Cool and freeze.

To serve, thaw chicken mixture, and cook rice according to package directions. Heat chicken mixture in a saucepan until bubbly, stir in drained orange segments, and heat through. Combine with cooked rice and serve. Makes 4 servings.

Summary of processes: Cut 1 pound chicken into chunks; slice 2 cups fresh mushrooms, ½ cup green onion bulbs

Freeze in: 4-cup container

Serve with: French-cut green beans, biscuits

CHICKEN SPAGHETTI

1 12-ounce package spaghetti (semolina)
1½ pounds boneless, skinless chicken breasts (3 cups cooked)
1 28-ounce can Italian-style or plain crushed tomatoes in puree
1 2-ounce jar pimientos
1 cup chopped green bell pepper
1 cup chopped celery
1 cup sliced fresh mushrooms
1½ cups chopped onion
1 3-ounce can sliced ripe olives
1 package dry spaghetti sauce seasoning
Salt and pepper to taste
2 cups grated low-fat cheddar cheese*

*C*ook spaghetti until al dente; drain. At the same time, cut chicken into 1-inch cubes; cook chicken in a small amount of water until no longer pink in the center. In a large pot, combine chicken with remaining ingredients except cheese. Bring mixture to a boil; reduce heat. Simmer for 15 minutes, stirring occasionally. Add cooked spaghetti to sauce. Cool and freeze in 16-cup container; tape 1-quart bag with cheese to container.

To prepare for serving, thaw cheese and spaghetti. Preheat oven to 325°; pour spaghetti into an oven-proof casserole dish and bake for 40 minutes. Top spaghetti with cheese; return spaghetti to oven for 5 minutes more or until cheese melts. Makes 10 servings.

Summary of processes: Cut 1½ pounds chicken into 1-inch cubes; chop 1 cup green bell pepper, 1 cup celery, and 1½ cups onion; slice 1 cup fresh mushrooms; grate 2 cups low-fat cheddar cheese

Freeze in: 16-cup container; 1-quart bag

Serve with: Tossed green salad, Cheesy-Herb Bread (page 180)

CHAPTER FOUR
Two-Week Entrée Plan B

$\mathcal{S}$he watches over the affairs
of her household and does not
eat the bread of idleness.

Proverbs 31:27

Menu
· C A L E N D A R ·

Sunday	Monday	Tuesday	Wednesday	Thursday	Friday	Saturday
	Eat Out Cooking Day! *1*	Herbed Chicken *2*	Biscuit Beef Bake *3*	French Stuffed Potatoes *4*	Chicken Nuggets *5*	Playoff Burgers *6*
Farmer's Casserole *7*	Poppy Turkey *8*	Crab Shells *9*	Country Captain *10*	Denise's Black Beans *11*	Spicy Garlic Chicken Pizza *12*	London Broil *13*
Mexican Chicken Lasagna *14*	Sopa de Maiz *15*	*16*	*17*	*18*	*19*	*20*
21	*22*	*23*	*24*	*25*	*26*	*27*
28	*29*	*30*				

GROCERY SHOPPING AND STAPLES LISTS

An asterisk(*) after an item indicates it can be stored until you cook that dish. For example, the can of mandarin oranges will not be needed until the day you serve Country Captain. Mark those items before you put them away as a reminder that you will need them for an entrée.

When entrées require perishable foods to be refrigerated until served, you may want to use those dishes right away or buy the food the week you plan to prepare the dish.

For two-week entrée Plan B you will need these food items as well as the ones on the staples list that follows.

GROCERY SHOPPING LIST

Canned Goods

1 4-ounce can mushroom stems and pieces

1 10¾-ounce can cream of mushroom soup

5 14½-ounce cans stewed tomatoes

1 14½-ounce can Mexican-style stewed tomatoes

2 8-ounce cans tomato sauce

1 15-ounce can tomato sauce

½ cup salsa, medium or mild

5 15-ounce cans black beans

2 4-ounce cans chopped green chilis

1 12-ounce can evaporated milk or evaporated skim milk

Grains, Pasta, and Rice

2 5.7-ounce boxes of couscous* (or enough to serve 6)

1 16-ounce (12-inch) Italian bread shell (Boboli brand)

32-ounce bag of rice*

2 10-ounce boxes uncooked lasagna noodles

8 ounces linguini

6 whole wheat buns or Kaiser rolls

12 jumbo pasta shells

Dry Ingredients and Seasonings

½ cup dried bread crumbs—Italian style

¼ cup slivered almonds

1 1¼-ounce package taco seasoning

1 10½-ounce bag of Fritos or corn chips*

Frozen Foods

2 16-ounce bags frozen corn

26-ounce bag frozen shredded hash brown potatoes

Dairy Products

2 sticks butter or margarine

1¼ cups grated Parmesan cheese

3 cups (12 ounces) grated Monterey Jack cheese

1 cup (4 ounces) Monterey Jack cheese with jalapeño peppers (also called hot pepper cheese)

2 ounces mozzarella cheese, grated

7 eggs

1 16-ounce container ricotta cheese

4½ cups milk

½ cup each grated Swiss and cheddar cheese

1 cup cottage cheese

1 8-ounce package light cream cheese

1 cup plain low-fat yogurt

1 12-ounce package Hungry Jack buttermilk biscuits*

1 cup of sour cream

Meat, Poultry, and Seafood

6 pounds boneless, skinless chicken breasts

5 to 6 pounds chicken pieces

2 pounds ground turkey

4 pounds lean ground beef

2 pounds London broil

⅓ pound fully cooked ham

1 pound smoked sausage links (i.e., Lit'l Smokies)

½ pound crabmeat or imitation crabmeat

Produce

5 to 6 large bunches green onions

11 cloves garlic

½ cup fresh parsley

¼ cup currants or raisins

4 medium yellow onions

1 tomato*

1 avocado*

4 large baking potatoes*

2 green bell peppers

1 bunch celery

1 lemon

STAPLES LIST

A-1 sauce

all-purpose flour

basil

bay leaves

black pepper

brown sugar

cayenne pepper

chili powder

cornstarch

cumin

curry powder

Dijon mustard

dried oregano leaves

dried thyme leaves

ground ginger

ground mace or nutmeg

chicken bouillon cubes (4)

onion salt

poppy seeds

salsa

salt

soy sauce

sugar

vegetable oil

white vinegar

Worcestershire sauce

FREEZER CONTAINERS

The following list of freezer containers or flat baking dishes will be needed for the entrées in two-week entrée plan B. They're not the only containers in which you could freeze these foods, but the list gives you an idea of the size and number of containers you'll need.

9 1-gallon freezer bags:
Chicken Nuggets, Spicy Garlic Chicken Pizza, Herbed Chicken, Country Captain, French Stuffed Potatoes, Poppy Turkey (2), Playoff Burgers, London Broil

5 1-quart freezer bags:
Chicken Nuggets, Spicy Garlic Chicken Pizza (2), French Stuffed Potatoes, Playoff Burgers

2 13x9x2-inch baking dishes:
Mexican Chicken Lasagna, Farmer's Casserole

1 10-inch round baking dish:
Crab Shells

1 5-cup container:
Biscuit Beef Bake

1 6-cup container:
Sopa de Maiz

1 10-cup container:
Denise's Black Beans

THE DAY BEFORE COOKING DAY

1. Store the Hungry Jack buttermilk biscuits, rice, couscous, Fritos, 1 tomato, 1 avocado, 4 large baking potatoes, and linguini in the refrigerator or cupboard until the day you will be serving the corresponding entrée. Be sure to label each so you won't forget and use them for other dishes.

2. Bring 3 pounds boneless, skinless chicken breasts to boil in a large pot in at least 6 cups of water. Boil gently until chicken is tender and no longer pink in the center—about 15 minutes. Drain, reserving 3 cups chicken broth. Chop the cooked chicken. Refrigerate until ready to use on cooking day.

3. Set out appliances, canned goods, dry ingredients, freezer containers, and recipes.

COOKING DAY ASSEMBLY ORDER

Make sure you've cleared the table and counters of unnecessary kitchenware to allow plenty of working room. It also helps to have fresh, damp washcloths and towels for wiping your hands and the cooking area. The day will go a lot smoother if you clean and organize as you work.

Before you prepare a recipe, gather all the spices and ingredients in the assembly area to save time and steps. When you finish the recipe, remove unneeded items and wipe off the work space.

BEFORE ASSEMBLING DISHES

1. Perform all chopping, crushing, grating, and slicing tasks.

Parsley: chop ¼ cup.

Celery: chop 1½ cups.

Green pepper: chop 2 cups.

Green onions: slice 5 to 6 large bunches to make 2½ cups.

Monterey Jack cheese with jalepeño peppers: grate 1 cup.

Mozzarella cheese: grate ½ cup.

Swiss cheese: grate ½ cup.

Lemon zest: grate 2 tablespoons.

Boneless chicken breasts: cube 3 pounds (use kitchen scissors for best results).

Ham: cube 1 cup.

Smoked sausage: slice 1 pound.
Onions: chop 3¾ cups.
Garlic: mince 10 cloves.

2. Assemble Denise's Black Beans in a slow cooker.

ASSEMBLE CHICKEN DISHES

1. Assemble Chicken Nuggets.

2. Assemble Spicy Garlic Chicken.

3. While chicken is marinating in refrigerator, assemble Herbed Chicken.

4. Assemble Country Captain.

5. Complete Spicy Garlic Chicken Pizza and freeze.

6. Assemble Mexican Chicken Lasagna.

7. Assemble Sopa de Maiz.

8. Label and freeze chicken dishes.

ASSEMBLE BEEF AND GROUND TURKEY DISHES

1. In 2 skillets, brown ground beef and onions for Biscuit Beef Bake, and ground beef for French Stuffed Potatoes. Finish one at a time.

2. Assemble Poppy Turkey.

3. Assemble Playoff Burgers.

4. Make sauce for London Broil.

5. Label and freeze beef and ground turkey dishes.

ASSEMBLE SEAFOOD AND MISCELLANEOUS DISHES

1. Assemble Crab Shells.

2. Assemble Farmer's Casserole.

3. Label and freeze these two dishes.

4. Cool Denise's Black Beans after they've cooked 8 hours. Label and freeze.

RECIPES FOR TWO-WEEK ENTRÉE PLAN B

Each recipe offers complete instructions on how to prepare the dish. Food items with an asterisk (*) won't be prepared until you serve the entrée. For recipes calling for oven baking, preheat oven for about 10 minutes.

"Summary of processes" gives a quick overview of foods that need to be chopped, diced, grated, or sliced. "Freeze in" tells what bags and containers will be needed to freeze each entrée. "Serve with" offers suggestions of foods to accompany the meal. Some of the recipes for those foods are included in chapter 8; page numbers are indicated for easy reference. "Note" includes special instructions on how the entrée can be used in other ways.

DENISE'S BLACK BEANS

1 pound smoked sausage cut into pieces (i.e., Lit'l Smokies)
3 15-ounce cans black beans, drained
1½ cups chopped onion
1½ cups chopped green bell pepper
1½ cups chopped celery
4 teaspoons minced garlic (4 cloves)
2 teaspoons dried thyme leaves
1½ teaspoons dried oregano leaves
1½ teaspoons pepper
¼ teaspoon cayenne pepper
1 chicken bouillon cube
5 bay leaves
1 8-ounce can tomato sauce
1 cup water
Rice* (to serve 8)

*C*ombine all ingredients, except rice, in a slow cooker. Cook on low for 8 hours. Remove bay leaves. Cool to room temperature and freeze.

When preparing to serve, heat to boiling and simmer 15 minutes. Serve over hot, cooked rice. Makes 8 servings.

Summary of processes: Chop 1½ cups onion, 1½ cups green pepper, and 1½ cups celery; mince 4 cloves garlic

Serve with: Rice, Blueberry Peach Fruit Crisp (page 193)

Freeze in: 1 6-cup container

CHICKEN NUGGETS

2 pounds boneless, skinless chicken breasts
3 tablespoons margarine or butter, melted
2 teaspoons Worcestershire sauce
½ cup dried bread crumbs—Italian style
⅓ cup grated Parmesan cheese

*C*ut chicken into 1-inch pieces (kitchen shears work best). Combine chicken, melted margarine, and Worcestershire in a 1-quart freezer bag. Combine the bread crumbs and Parmesan cheese in a second freezer bag. Tape the two bags together. Label and freeze.

To prepare for serving, thaw and remove the chicken pieces from marinade. Shake them in the bread crumb bag to coat, a few at a time. Preheat oven to 450°. Arrange chicken on a greased cookie sheet. Bake for 7 to 9 minutes or until no longer pink in the center. Makes 4 servings.

Summary of processes: Cut 2 pounds boneless, skinless chicken into 1-inch pieces

Freeze in: 1-gallon bag; 1-quart bag

Serve with: Chips and dips; green bean casserole; catsup or barbecue sauce for dipping

RECIPES

SPICY GARLIC CHICKEN PIZZA

12 ounces boneless, skinless chicken breasts
½ cup sliced green onion, divided
2 cloves garlic, minced
2 tablespoons white vinegar
2 tablespoons soy sauce
3 tablespoons vegetable oil, divided
¼ teaspoon cayenne pepper
¼ teaspoon black pepper
1 tablespoon water
1 tablespoon cornstarch
1 16-ounce (12-inch) Italian bread shell (Boboli brand)
½ cup grated Monterey Jack cheese
½ cup grated mozzarella cheese
¼ cup slivered almonds

Cut chicken into 1-inch pieces (kitchen shears work best). In a large bowl combine green onion, minced garlic, vinegar, soy sauce, 2 tablespoons oil, and the cayenne and black pepper. Add the chicken pieces; stir to coat. Refrigerate the chicken in the soy sauce for 30 minutes. Drain, reserving marinade.

Heat remaining oil in a large skillet on medium high; add chicken pieces. Cook and stir about 5 to 7 minutes or until no longer pink. Add 1 tablespoon water and stir cornstarch into reserved marinade. Add to skillet. Cook and stir until thickened and bubbly. Cool and freeze. While chicken is cooking, combine the grated cheeses in a 1-quart bag, the remaining green onions in a 1-quart bag and the nuts in another 1-quart bag. Tape all three bags together to the package of the Italian bread shell.

To prepare for serving, thaw chicken mixture. Preheat oven to 400°. Spoon mixture evenly atop bread shell. Sprinkle with cheese. Bake, uncovered, for 12 minutes. Top with slivered almonds. Return to oven for 2 minutes more. Makes 4 servings.

Summary of processes: Cut 12 ounces boneless, skinless chicken into 1-inch pieces; slice ½ cup green onion; mince 2 cloves garlic; grate ½ cup Monterey Jack cheese and ½ cup mozzarella cheese

Freeze in: 1-gallon bag; 2 1-quart bags

Serve with: Spinach salad with creamy mustard dressing

HERBED CHICKEN

2½ to 3 pounds chicken pieces
1 10¾-ounce can cream of mushroom soup
1 teaspoon grated lemon zest
1½ tablespoons lemon juice
½ teaspoon salt
1 teaspoon dried basil leaves
1 teaspoon dried oregano leaves
Rice* (to serve 6)

*P*lace chicken in a 1-gallon freezer bag. In a small bowl, combine the remaining ingredients, except rice. Pour over the chicken and freeze.

To prepare for serving, thaw chicken mixture. Preheat oven to 350°. Place mixture in a 13x9x2-inch baking dish, treated with nonstick spray. Cover and bake for 1¼ hours. Serve over hot, cooked rice. Makes 6 servings.

Summary of processes: Grate 1 tablespoon lemon zest

Freeze in: 1-gallon bag

Serve with: French-cut green beans

COUNTRY CAPTAIN

1 14½-ounce can stewed tomatoes (undrained)
¼ cup fresh parsley, chopped
¼ cup currants or raisins
1 tablespoon curry powder
½ chicken bouillon cube
½ teaspoon ground mace or nutmeg
¼ teaspoon sugar
1 teaspoon salt
2½ to 3 pounds chicken pieces
1 tablespoon cornstarch
1 tablespoon cold water
Hot cooked couscous* (to serve 6)

*I*n a medium bowl, stir together tomatoes, parsley, currants or raisins, curry powder, bouillon cube, mace or nutmeg, sugar, and salt. Pour over chicken in freezer bag. Label and freeze.

To prepare for serving, place thawed chicken and sauce in large skillet. Bring mixture to boiling; reduce heat. Cover and simmer for 20 minutes or until chicken is no longer pink. Remove chicken from skillet; keep warm. Skim fat from mixture in skillet. In a small bowl stir together cornstarch and cold water; add to skillet. Cook and stir till thickened and bubbly. Cook and stir 2 minutes more. Serve over couscous or hot rice. Sprinkle with almonds, if desired. Makes 6 servings.

Summary of processes: Chop ¼ cup fresh parsley

Freeze in: 1-gallon bag; 1-quart bag

Serve with: Tropical fruit, crescent rolls

MEXICAN CHICKEN LASAGNA

¾ cup chopped onion
3 14-ounce cans stewed tomatoes with juice
½ cup salsa, medium or mild
1 1¼-ounce package taco seasoning
1 16-ounce can black beans, rinsed and drained
1 large egg
16 ounces ricotta cheese
2 teaspoons minced garlic (2 cloves)
10 uncooked lasagna noodles
4 boneless, skinless cooked chicken breasts (about 1 pound) cut into
    1-inch cubes
1 4-ounce can chopped green chilies
1½ cups (about 6 ounces) grated Monterey Jack cheese

*T*o make sauce, combine chopped onion with tomatoes, salsa, and taco seasoning. Stir in beans.

To make ricotta layer, whisk egg in small bowl with a fork. Whisk in ricotta cheese and garlic.

Spread 1 cup tomato sauce mixture over the bottom of a greased 13x9x2-inch casserole dish (should barely cover bottom). Top with 5 (uncooked) noodles, overlapping slightly. Spread on one half of the ricotta cheese mixture. Sprinkle with half the chicken and half the chilies. Spoon 2 cups tomato sauce mixture on top, then add the rest of the ricotta cheese mixture; spread lightly. Sprinkle with half the grated cheese. Top with remaining noodles, chicken, chilies, tomato sauce mixture, and grated cheese. Cover with foil, label and freeze.

To prepare for serving, thaw and preheat oven to 350°. Bake, uncovered, for 40 minutes or until noodles are tender when pierced with sharp knife. Cool 10 minutes before serving. Makes 8 servings.

Summary of processes: Chop ¾ cup onion; mince 2 cloves garlic; cut 4 boneless, skinless cooked chicken breasts into 1-inch cubes; seed 4 ounces whole green chilies and slice into thin strips; grate 1½ cups Monterey jack cheese

Freeze in: 13x9x2-inch baking dish

Serve with: Slices of avocado and pink grapefruit on lettuce with poppyseed dressing

SOPA DE MAIZ

2 cups chicken broth
2 boneless, skinless cooked chicken breasts, chopped
1 16-ounce bag frozen corn
½ teaspoon cumin
1 teaspoon minced garlic (1 clove)
2 chicken bouillon cubes
1 4-ounce can diced green chilies
1 cup milk
Salt and pepper to taste
Fritos*
1 tomato, chopped*
1 avocado, chopped*
Salsa
Sour cream

*C*ombine first 7 ingredients in a 6-cup container and freeze.

When preparing to serve, thaw the soup and bring just to boiling. Add milk and simmer until soup is heated through. Season with salt and pepper.

In individual bowls, layer crushed Fritos, chopped tomatoes, and diced avocados. Then pour soup over all. Add dollop each of salsa and sour cream. Makes 5 to 6 servings.

Summary of processes: Chop 2 boneless, skinless cooked chicken breasts

Freeze in: 6-cup container

Serve with: Taco salad

BISCUIT BEEF BAKE

1 pound lean ground beef
½ cup onion, chopped
1 teaspoon minced garlic (1 clove)
1 14½ ounce can Mexican-style stewed tomatoes, undrained
1 15-ounce can black beans, rinsed and drained
1 8-ounce can tomato sauce
½ cup frozen corn
2 teaspoons chili powder
1 teaspoon cumin
1 teaspoon salt
1 12-ounce package Hungry Jack buttermilk biscuits*

*B*rown ground beef with the onion and garlic in a 10-inch skillet over medium heat until meat is no longer pink (or use 2½ cups already-browned ground beef). Stir in the remaining ingredients, except biscuits. Bring to a boil and simmer for 10 minutes. Cool. Package, label, and freeze. Store the tube of Hungry Jack biscuits in the refrigerator.

When preparing to serve, thaw and preheat oven to 400°. Transfer the mixture to an 8x8-inch ovenproof dish that has been treated with nonstick spray. Arrange the biscuits on top and bake for 15 to 20 minutes. Makes 6 servings.

Summary of processes: Chop ½ cup onion; mince 1 clove garlic

Freeze in: 5-cup container

Serve with: Baked apples

RECIPES

FRENCH STUFFED POTATOES

1 pound lean ground beef
¼ cup chopped green onion
1 4-ounce can mushroom stems and pieces
½ teaspoon salt
½ teaspoon onion salt
½ cup each grated Swiss and cheddar cheese
4 large baking potatoes*

*B*rown together in a skillet the ground beef, green onion, and mushrooms (add a tablespoon of water if mixture is too dry). Add the salt and onion salt.

Freeze the meat mixture in a freezer bag. Store the grated cheese in a small bag and slip the smaller bag into the larger one; store in freezer. Store the potatoes in the pantry (don't freeze raw potatoes).

When preparing to serve, thaw the meat mixture and cheeses. Preheat oven to 400°. Bake the potatoes for 1 hour or until done. When potatoes are nearly done, heat the meat mixture in a small saucepan or skillet.

Slice open the potatoes, break up potatoes with a fork, and spoon the meat mixture and cheese atop each potato. Return to the oven until cheese is melted. Makes 4 servings.

Summary of processes: Chop ¼ cup green onions; grate ½ cup cheddar cheese and ½ cup Swiss cheese.

Freeze in: 1-gallon bag; 1-quart bag

Serve with: Sliced tomatoes, Caesar salad

POPPY TURKEY

2 pounds ground turkey
½ cup chopped green pepper
½ teaspoon salt
½ cup chopped onion
1 15-ounce can tomato sauce
1 cup low-fat cottage cheese
1 tablespoon poppy seed
1 cup plain low-fat yogurt
1 8-ounce package light cream cheese
¼ teaspoon pepper
8 ounces linguini*
¼ cup grated Parmesan cheese*

Sauté the turkey with green pepper, salt, and onion in a large skillet on medium heat until the turkey is no longer pink. Add tomato sauce and set aside. Combine the remaining ingredients in a medium bowl, except linguini and Parmesan cheese. Freeze each of the two mixtures in 1-gallon bags taped together.

When preparing to serve, thaw the bags. Preheat oven to 350°. Cook 8 ounces linguini according to package directions and drain. While pasta is hot, mix it into the cheese mixture in a medium bowl. Spread the linguini and cheese on the bottom of a greased casserole dish. Top with the meat mixture and sprinkle with Parmesan cheese. Bake for 30 minutes or until hot and bubbly. Makes 10 servings.

Summary of processes: Chop ½ cup green pepper and ½ cup onion

Freeze in: 2 1-gallon bags

Serve with: Green beans, Cheesy-Herb Bread (page 180)

RECIPES

PLAYOFF BURGERS

2 pounds lean ground beef
1 onion, chopped
1 tablespoon A-1 sauce
¼ pound grated Monterey Jack cheese
Salt and pepper to taste
6 whole wheat buns *

*S*alt and pepper ground beef to taste and mix with chopped onion and A-1 sauce. Make 12 thin patties. Sprinkle cheese over 6 of these, then top with remaining 6 patties and press edges together. Wrap each patty in waxed paper and seal them in a 1-gallon freezer bag. Slip inside the bag a 1-quart freezer bag. Label the bag and freeze. Freeze the package of whole wheat buns.

To prepare for serving, thaw patties and place on the rack of a broiler pan. Broil 3 to 4 inches from the heat for a total of 12 to 14 minutes or until done, turning once. Serve on thawed whole wheat buns, split and toasted. Makes 6 servings.

Summary of processes: Chop one onion

Freeze in: 1-gallon bag

Serve with: Carrot sticks, baked beans, watermelon

Note: Great on the grill or for camping trips.

LONDON BROIL

1 London Broil or flank steak (about 2 pounds)
1 teaspoon ground ginger
1 tablespoon grated lemon zest
1 tablespoon vegetable oil
1 clove garlic, minced
1 teaspoon black pepper
1 teaspoon brown sugar

*I*n a shallow bowl, large enough to hold the steak, stir all other ingredients together, making a marinade. Turn the steak in the marinade, rubbing the ingredients into the meat. Put steak in a freezer bag; label and freeze.

To prepare for serving, thaw steak. Grill over hot coals 4 to 5 minutes per side. Do not overcook or flank steak becomes tough (serving rare is best). Makes 5 servings.

Freeze in: 1-cup freezer container

Serve with: Baked potato, Fresh-Baked Asparagus (page 200)

RECIPES

FARMER'S CASSEROLE

6 cups frozen shredded hash brown potatoes
1 cup grated Monterey Jack cheese with jalapeño peppers
1 cup diced fully cooked ham
¼ cup sliced green onion
4 beaten eggs
1 12-ounce can evaporated milk or evaporated skim milk (1½ cups)
⅛ teaspoon pepper
¼ teaspoon salt

*G*rease a 13x9x2-inch baking dish. Arrange potatoes evenly in the bottom of the dish. Sprinkle with cheese, ham, and green onion.

In a medium mixing bowl combine eggs, milk, pepper, and salt. Pour egg mixture over potato mixture in dish. Freeze.

To prepare to serve, thaw and preheat oven to 350°. Bake, uncovered, for 40 to 45 minutes or until center appears set. Let stand 5 minutes before serving. Makes 12 servings.

Summary of processes: Grate 1 cup Monterey Jack cheese with jalapeño peppers; dice 1 cup ham; slice ¼ cup green onions

Freeze in: 13x9x2-inch baking dish

Serve with: Wedges of cantaloupe, Apple-Date Freezer Coffee Cake (page 186)

CHAPTER FOUR

CRAB SHELLS

6 tablespoons butter or margarine, divided
3 green onions, chopped (½ cup)
½ teaspoon Worcestershire sauce
1 teaspoon Dijon mustard
½ pound crab meat (or imitation), chopped small
Salt and pepper to taste
12 jumbo pasta shells
4 tablespoons all-purpose flour
2½ cups milk
½ cup grated Parmesan cheese, divided

*I*n a small saucepan or skillet melt 2 tablespoons of butter. Add chopped green onion, Worcestershire sauce, mustard, crab meat, and salt and pepper to taste. Stir over medium heat until heated through. Fill pasta shells with mixture and arrange shells in round baking dish that has been treated with nonstick spray.

In same skillet melt 4 tablespoons butter. Stir in flour. Remove from heat and gradually whisk in milk. Return to a boil and cook for 3 minutes, stirring. Stir in salt and pepper and ¼ cup of the Parmesan cheese, stirring till the cheese melts. Pour sauce over shells and top with remaining cheese. Cover with foil; label and freeze.

To prepare for serving, thaw and preheat oven to 400°. Cover and bake for 30 minutes. Makes 4 to 5 servings.

Summary of processes: Chop 3 green onions and crab meat

Freeze in: 10-inch round baking dish

Serve with: Cucumber salad

RECIPES

CHAPTER FIVE
One-Month Entrée Plan A

*S*he is like the merchant ships,
bringing her food from afar. She
gets up while it is still dark; she
provides food for her family and
portions for her servant girls.

Proverbs 31:14–15

Menu

· C A L E N D A R ·

Sunday	Monday	Tuesday	Wednesday	Thursday	Friday	Saturday
	Eat Out Cooking Day! 1	Manicotti 2	Chinese Chicken Morsels 3	Veal Scallopini in Spaghetti Sauce 4	Teriyaki Burgers 5	Ham and Swiss Pastry Bake 6
Baked Eggs 7	Cheesy Corn Casserole 8	Poulet de France 9	Mimi's Chicken Soup 10	Joes to Go 11	Winter Barley 12	Bacon-Wrapped Burgers 13
Meal-in-One Potatoes 14	Hot Brisket Sandwiches 15	Spaghetti 16	Chicken Packets 17	Aztec Quiche 18	Wild Rice Chicken 19	Taco Pie 20
Linguine à la Anne 21	Stove-Top Barbecued Chicken 22	French Bread Pizza 23	Ham Dinner Slices 24	Ravioli Soup 25	Heavenly Chicken 26	Mrs. Ringle's Brisket 27
Baked Herb Fish Fillets 28	Teriyaki Chicken 29	Fruity Curried Chicken 30				

GROCERY SHOPPING AND STAPLES LISTS

An asterisk (*) after an item indicates that it can be stored until you cook the dish it will be served with. For example, the spaghetti noodles will not be cooked until the day you serve Spaghetti. Mark those items as a reminder that you'll need them for an entrée.

When entrées require perishable foods to be refrigerated until served, you may want to use those dishes right away or buy the food the week you plan to prepare the dish. For example, fresh mushrooms would spoil by the end of a month.

For one-month entrée plan A, you will need these food items as well as the ones in the staples list that follows.

GROCERY SHOPPING LIST

Canned Goods

1 8¾-ounce can apricots

1 14½-ounce can beef broth

1 8-ounce bottle chili sauce

2 10¾-ounce cans condensed cream of mushroom soup (1 can*)

1 12-ounce can evaporated skim milk

2 4-ounce cans diced, green chilies

1 15-ounce can red kidney beans

1 17-ounce can whole kernel corn

1 2-ounce and 1 4-ounce can mushroom stems and pieces

1 15-ounce can chopped tomatoes

4 28-ounce cans Italian-style or plain crushed tomatoes in puree

1 12-ounce and 1 6-ounce can tomato paste

3 8-ounce cans tomato sauce

1 8-ounce can sliced water chestnuts

Grains, Pasta, and Rice

7 bread slices

1 loaf unsliced French bread (not sourdough)*

6 hamburger buns*

8 to 10 sandwich rolls*

1 8-ounce container Italian-flavored bread crumbs*

1 12-ounce package linguine

1 8-ounce package manicotti

1 16-ounce package spaghetti*

1 8-ounce package spinach or wide egg noodles*

1 8-ounce package tortellini*

1 12-ounce package seasoned bread stuffing—7-pound bird size (6 cups)

1 6¼-ounce package long grain and wild rice (Uncle Ben's Fast Cooking Long Grain and Wild Rice, if available)

1 32-ounce package regular rice

Quick-cooking barley (need ¾ cup)

Dry Ingredients and Seasonings

⅓ cup raisins

1 1½-ounce package onion soup mix

1 1¼-ounce taco seasoning mix

About 1½ cups seasoned croutons (1 cup croutons, ½ cup crushed)

Frozen Foods

4 frozen fish fillets (about 1¼ pounds) orange roughy or sole

2 9-inch deep-dish frozen pie shells (1*)

1 12-ounce package plain ravioli without sauce* (located in the frozen or refrigerated section)

1 10-ounce package frozen, chopped spinach

Dairy Products

About 1 cup (2 sticks) margarine

1 8-ounce carton small curd, low-fat cottage cheese with chives

1 16-ounce carton small curd, low-fat cottage cheese

2 8-ounce packages refrigerated crescent rolls*

19 eggs

1 cup half-and-half

2 quarts milk

18 ounces (4½ cups) grated mild cheddar cheese

1 3-ounce package cream cheese

5 ounces (1¼ cups) grated Monterey Jack cheese

16 ounces (4 cups) mozzarella cheese (4 remaining slices, grated)

12 ounces (about 3 cups) grated Parmesan cheese

1 15-ounce container part-skim ricotta cheese

2 ounces (½ cup) grated Romano cheese

4 ounces (1 cup) grated Swiss cheese

1 8-ounce carton sour cream

Meat and Poultry

1 4-to-6-pound beef brisket

8 pounds lean ground beef (This allows 1 pound for hamburgers; buy more if needed for your family.)

½ pound freshly ground turkey

9 pounds whole chickens or 7 pounds breasts

5¾ pounds boneless, skinless chicken breasts

2 pounds chicken pieces (breasts, drumsticks, or thighs)

4 strips bacon

5 to 6 pounds boneless, cooked ham, with 3 pounds cubed, and the center portion cut in dinner slices

1 pound bulk Italian sausage

1 pound very thin, boneless veal cutlets* (or substitute 1 pound boneless, skinless chicken breasts)

3-ounce package (use ½) sliced pepperoni

Produce

3 medium carrots

1 bunch celery

1 whole head garlic (10 cloves)

1 small lemon*

1 small head of lettuce

1 small bunch green onions

2 medium green bell peppers

1 red bell pepper

6 pounds (about 9) yellow onions

1 bunch fresh parsley

1 bunch chives

STAPLES LIST

Make sure you have the following staples on hand; add those you don't have to the above shopping list:

dried basil leaves

bay leaves

biscuit baking mix (1 cup)

brown sugar (about ¾ cup)

catsup (⅓ cup)

cayenne pepper

celery seed

chicken bouillon cube

chili powder

ground cinnamon

cloves (whole)

ground cumin

curry powder

all-purpose flour

garlic powder

garlic salt

ground ginger

lemon juice (about ⅔ cup)

lemon pepper

marjoram

light mayonnaise (about 2 cups)

minced onion

Dijon mustard (¼ cup)

dry mustard (1 teaspoon)
prepared mustard
nonstick spray
onion salt
dried oregano leaves
pepper
8 medium baking potatoes*
8 to 10 new potatoes*
salt
soda crackers (1 cup crumbs)
soy sauce (¾ cup)
sugar
dried thyme leaves
3 tomatoes*
vegetable oil
red wine vinegar
white vinegar
waxed paper
Worcestershire sauce

FREEZER CONTAINERS

The following list of freezer containers or flat baking dishes will be needed for the entrées. These are not the only containers you could use, but this list gives you an idea of the size and number of containers you'll need.

Heavy aluminum foil:
French Bread Pizza

15 1-quart freezer bags:
French Bread Pizza (3), Linguine à la Anne (2), Chicken Packets (2), Veal Scallopini in Spaghetti Sauce (2), Heavenly Chicken, Poulet de France, Taco Pie, Cheesy Corn Casserole, Meal-in-One Potatoes, Baked Herb Fish Fillets

13 1-gallon freezer bags:
Mrs. Ringle's Brisket, Hot Brisket Sandwiches, Veal Scallopini, Ham and Swiss Pastry Bake, Wild Rice Chicken, Chinese Chicken Morsels, Bacon-Wrapped Burgers, Ham Dinner Slices, Teriyaki Burgers, Teriyaki Chicken, Baked Herb Fish Fillets, Stove-Top Barbecued Chicken, Winter Barley

1 4-cup container:
Spaghetti Sauce

2 3-cup containers:
Veal Scallopini in Spaghetti Sauce, French Bread Pizza

1 4-cup container:
Fruity Curried Chicken

2 8-cup containers:
Joes to Go, Mimi's Chicken Soup

1 10-cup container:
Ravioli Soup

1 8x8x2-inch baking dish:
Cheesy Corn Casserole

4 13x9x2-inch baking dishes:
Linguine à la Anne, Heavenly Chicken, Poulet de France, Baked Eggs

1 3-quart casserole of any shape:
Manicotti

1 9-inch quiche or pie pan:
Aztec Quiche

1 10-inch quiche or pie pan:
Taco Pie

THE DAY BEFORE COOKING DAY

1. Cut 1½ pounds of boneless chicken breasts into 1-inch cubes with kitchen scissors and refrigerate. Refrigerate remaining boneless chicken breasts and 2 pounds of chicken pieces.

2. Refrigerate lemon, and store baking and new potatoes until you're ready to serve them.

3. Place 9 pounds whole chickens (or 7 pounds breasts) in about 6 quarts water in a large pot (may need two). Bring to a boil; reduce heat. Cover and simmer until thickest pieces are done, about 45 minutes to 1 hour. Save and refrigerate 3¼ quarts chicken broth. Cool chicken until ready to handle. Remove meat from bones and skin. Cut chicken into bite-size pieces using kitchen scissors, which are easier to use than a knife. Refrigerate chicken pieces in two plastic bags.

4. Put ham dinner slices, hamburger buns, and sandwich rolls in freezer bags; mark bags with names of recipes; store them in freezer until ready to serve.

5. For Veal Scallopini in Spaghetti Sauce, put veal cutlets in 1-gallon bag, Italian-flavored bread crumbs and mozzarella cheese in separate 1-quart bags; freeze them together.

6. For French Bread Pizza, put pepperoni in 1-quart freezer bag, ¼ cup grated Parmesan cheese and 1 cup grated mozzarella cheese in separate 1-quart freezer bags; wrap French bread in heavy foil, and put them together in freezer.

7. Set out appliances, bowls, canned goods, dry ingredients, freezer containers, and recipes.

8. Start Mrs. Ringle's Brisket in a Crockpot (just before bed).

COOKING DAY ASSEMBLY ORDER

Make sure you've cleared the table and counters of unnecessary kitchenware to allow plenty of working room. It also helps to have fresh, damp washcloths and towels for wiping your hands and the cooking area. The day will go a lot smoother if you clean and organize as you work.

Before you prepare a recipe, gather all the spices and ingredients in the assembly area to save time and steps. When you finish the recipe, remove unneeded items and wipe off the work space.

BEFORE ASSEMBLING DISHES

1. Cool, slice, and divide brisket and gravy in half for Mrs. Ringle's Brisket and Hot Brisket Sandwiches. Put brisket in two 1-gallon bags and freeze them. Wash out Crockpot.

2. Skim and discard fat from chicken broth.

3. Perform all chopping, crushing, grating, and slicing tasks.

> Ham: cut 8 cups into cubes.
>
> Onions: leave one onion whole for Mimi's Chicken Soup; finely chop remaining onions. Open windows, and keep tissues handy. Store onions in cold water in a container with a tight lid.
>
> Green onions: chop ½ cup.
>
> Green bell peppers: finely chop 1; slice 1.
>
> Red bell pepper: slice 1.
>
> Carrots: shred 3.
>
> Celery: slice ½ cup with leaves; finely chop 1¾ cups.
>
> Garlic: mince 8½ teaspoons (8½ cloves).
>
> Parsley: chop ⅔ cup.
>
> Mozzarella cheese: cut 4 slices; grate the rest.
>
> Monterey Jack cheese: grate all.
>
> Mild cheddar cheese: grate all.
>
> Cracker crumbs: crush 1 cup.

4. Start Spaghetti Sauce.

5. Spray pans or baking dishes you will need with nonstick spray (check list of freezer containers on pages 97–98).

6. As you assemble the ham, chicken, beef, and miscellaneous entrées, allow them to cool if necessary, put them in storage containers, and freeze.

ASSEMBLE HAM DISHES

1. Boil linguine according to the package directions, setting timer.

2. Finish preparing Linguine à la Anne.

3. Assemble Ham and Swiss Pastry Bake.

4. Freeze ham dishes.

ASSEMBLE POULTRY DISHES

1. Prepare Stove-Top Barbecued Chicken in a skillet and simmer.

2. In separate saucepans, cook rice for Wild Rice Chicken and ¾ cup regular rice for Fruity Curried Chicken according to package directions.

3. Make filling for Chicken Packets in a medium bowl (mixing with hands works best), and put in a freezer bag.

4. Finish assembling Wild Rice Chicken and Fruity Curried Chicken.

5. Prepare Heavenly Chicken.

6. Prepare Chinese Chicken Morsels.

7. Assemble Poulet de France.

8. Assemble filling for Meal-in-One Potatoes.

9. Assemble Teriyaki Chicken.

10. Prepare Mimi's Chicken Soup with remaining chicken broth and start simmering.

11. Freeze poultry dishes.

ASSEMBLE MISCELLANEOUS DISHES

1. Prepare Baked Herb Fish Fillets coating mix.

2. Complete Aztec Quiche.

3. Prepare Baked Eggs. (If you use bacon for Baked Eggs, at the same time you fry it, fry 5 more slices till limp, and set aside for Bacon-Wrapped Burgers.)

4. Cool Spaghetti Sauce.

5. Freeze miscellaneous dishes.

ASSEMBLE BEEF DISHES

1. Cook manicotti according to package directions.

CHAPTER FIVE

2. Assemble Teriyaki Burgers.

3. Complete Bacon-Wrapped Burgers.

4. Drain manicotti; rinse with cold water. Separate manicotti noodles; put each on waxed paper.

5. In a large skillet, cook and stir 6 pounds lean ground beef until brown.

6. In a small skillet, sauté ⅓ and ¾ cups chopped onions until tender; use for Taco Pie and Joes to Go.

7. Assemble Ravioli Soup, starting it to simmer.

8. Finish Manicotti.

9. Put Spaghetti Sauce in freezer containers according to directions. Put containers of sauce for Veal Scallopini in Spaghetti Sauce and French Bread Pizza in freezer with already-packaged items for those dishes.

10. Assemble Taco Pie.

11. Prepare Joes to Go and Winter Barley.

12. Complete Cheesy Corn Casserole.

13. Allow Mimi's Chicken Soup and Ravioli Soup to cool, and store in freezer containers.

14. Freeze beef dishes.

You made it! Hooray!!

RECIPES FOR ONE-MONTH ENTRÉE PLAN A

Each recipe offers complete instructions on how to prepare the dish. Food items with an asterisk (*) won't be prepared until you serve the entrée. For recipes calling for oven baking, preheat oven for about 10 minutes.

"Summary of processes" gives a quick overview of foods that need to be chopped, diced, grated, or sliced. "Freeze in" tells what bags and containers will be needed to freeze each entrée. "Serve with" offers suggestions of foods to accompany the meal. Some of the recipes for those foods are included in chapter 8; page numbers are indicated for easy reference. "Note" includes special instructions on how the entrée can be used in other ways.

MRS. RINGLE'S BRISKET

1 4-to-6 pound brisket
2 tablespoons prepared mustard
1 package onion soup mix
4 to 5 new potatoes*

*P*lace brisket fat side up in a Crockpot. Do not add any water or liquid. Cover brisket with mustard and dry onion soup mix. Cook on low overnight.

Skim mustard and onion seasoning from brisket; mix with liquid. Remove brisket from Crockpot; allow to cool. Peel off fat and discard it; slice or shred meat. Save juices and seasonings (thicken with flour to make gravy if desired). Divide meat and gravy in half and store in separate 1-gallon bags in freezer. Reserve 1 bag for Mrs. Ringle's Brisket and one for Hot Brisket Sandwiches.

To prepare for serving, thaw brisket and gravy, and heat. At the same time, prepare new potatoes. Heat 1 cup salted water to a boil; add potatoes. Cover and heat till boiling; reduce heat. Simmer tightly covered until tender, 20 to 25 minutes; drain. Serve potatoes with brisket and gravy. Makes 4 to 5 servings.

Freeze in: 2 1-gallon bags

Serve with: Cheese grits, Cranberry Cream Salad (page 196)

HOT BRISKET SANDWICHES

Half of gravy and sliced brisket
4 to 6 sandwich rolls
Margarine or mayonnaise for rolls

*T*haw brisket slices; heat them in the gravy. Serve on warm sandwich rolls. Serve gravy on the side for dipping. Makes 4 to 6 servings.

Serve with: Cinnamon Applesauce Salad (page 197), celery slices

FRENCH BREAD PIZZA

1 loaf unsliced French bread (not sourdough)*
3 cups Spaghetti Sauce*
¼ cup grated Parmesan cheese*
1 cup grated mozzarella cheese*
3 ounces pepperoni slices (half a package)*

*T*his recipe is assembled on the day it's served. Put sauce in a 3-cup container, cheeses in 2 1-quart bags, pepperoni in 1-quart bag; wrap bread in heavy foil. Freeze them together.

To prepare for serving, thaw French bread, sauce, grated cheeses, and pepperoni. Slice loaf of French bread in half lengthwise. Layer sauce, Parmesan cheese, pepperoni, and mozzarella cheese on each half. Set oven to broil and/or 550°. Place bread on baking sheet, and put in the oven. Broil until mozzarella is melted. Cut into serving-size pieces. Makes 6 to 8 servings.

Summary of processes: Grate 4 ounces mozzarella cheese

Freeze in: 3-cup container; 3 1-quart bags; foil for bread

Serve with: Waldorf salad

SPAGHETTI SAUCE

1 pound bulk Italian sausage
1½ cups finely chopped onion
1 12-ounce can tomato paste
3 28-ounce cans Italian-style or plain crushed tomatoes in puree
2 cups water
4 teaspoons minced garlic (4 cloves)
4 bay leaves
2 tablespoons sugar
4 teaspoons dried basil leaves
2 teaspoons dried oregano leaves
4 tablespoons chopped fresh parsley
2 teaspoons salt
1 16-ounce package spaghetti*

*I*n a large pot, cook and stir the bulk Italian sausage with onions until the meat is brown; drain fat. Add remaining ingredients, except the spaghetti. Bring sauce to a boil; reduce heat. Partly cover, and simmer for 2 hours, stirring occasionally. (If desired, simmer in a Crockpot instead of pot.) Makes 12 cups sauce.

Allow sauce to cool. Freeze in separate containers for Spaghetti (4 cups); Veal Scallopini in Spaghetti Sauce (2½ cups); and French Bread Pizza (3 cups). Reserve 2½ cups sauce for Manicotti.

To prepare Spaghetti, thaw 4 cups sauce, and heat in a medium saucepan. At the same time, cook noodles according to package directions, drain, and pour sauce over them. Makes 6 servings.

Summary of processes: Chop 1½ cups onion, 4 tablespoons parsley; mince 4 cloves garlic

Freeze in: 4-cup container, Spaghetti; 2 3-cup containers, French Bread Pizza and Veal Scallopini in Spaghetti Sauce; reserve 2½ cups for Manicotti

Serve with: Jiffy Salad (page 196), garlic bread

VEAL SCALLOPINI IN SPAGHETTI SAUCE

1 pound thin veal cutlets (or substitute 1 pound boneless, skinless
　　chicken breasts)*
2½ cups Spaghetti Sauce*
1 egg*
¾ cup Italian-flavored bread crumbs*
3 tablespoons vegetable or olive oil*
1 teaspoon minced garlic (1 clove)*
4 slices mozzarella cheese*
Grated Parmesan cheese*

*T*his recipe is assembled on the day it's served. Put veal cutlets in 1-gallon bag, Spaghetti Sauce in a 3-cup container, Italian-flavored bread crumbs and mozzarella cheese in separate 1-quart bags; freeze them together.

　　Thaw veal cutlets, bread crumbs, cheese slices, and container of Spaghetti Sauce. Beat egg with fork until white and yolk are blended. Sprinkle Italian-flavored bread crumbs on a sheet of waxed paper. Dip veal into egg and then crumbs, turning to coat both sides evenly.

　　In a large skillet, heat oil with garlic over medium or medium-high heat. Add veal; sauté 4 minutes on each side, until golden brown. Top each piece of veal with a cheese slice. Pour Spaghetti Sauce around veal. Bring sauce to boil; reduce heat. Cover and simmer 5 minutes or until cheese is melted. Sprinkle Parmesan cheese on top. Makes 4 servings.

Summary of processes: Mince 1 clove garlic; slice 4 slices mozzarella cheese

Freeze in: 3-cup container, 1-gallon bag, and 2 1-quart bags

Serve with: Tossed green salad, Dawn's French Bread (page 183)

LINGUINE À LA ANNE

1 12-ounce package linguine
2 tablespoons margarine
2 tablespoons all-purpose flour
½ teaspoon salt
1 12-ounce can evaporated skim milk
1 4-ounce can mushroom stems and pieces, save liquid
1⅓ cups water
1 chicken bouillon cube
4 cups cooked, cubed ham
½ cup grated Romano cheese
1 sliced red bell pepper
1 sliced green bell pepper
1 tablespoon vegetable oil
1 cup seasoned croutons*

*C*ook linguine in a large pot according to package directions, drain, and return to pot. While linguine cooks, melt margarine in a medium saucepan over low heat. Stir in flour and salt, adding evaporated milk. Bring to a boil, stirring constantly. Boil and stir 1 minute. Add liquid from mushrooms, water, and bouillon cube. Cook over medium heat, stirring constantly, until bubbly and slightly thickened.

Add 2 cups sauce and drained mushrooms to linguine, and toss until well mixed. Spoon linguine mixture into a 13x9x2-inch baking dish that has been treated with nonstick spray, pressing linguine mixture up the sides to leave a slight hollow in center of dish.

Toss ham in remaining sauce; spread it in the center of the linguine. Sprinkle with Romano cheese; cover with foil, and freeze dish. Sauté red and green bell peppers in vegetable oil until soft; allow to cool. Put peppers in 1-quart freezer bag; attach this bag and croutons in a 1-quart freezer bag to the dish.

To prepare for serving, thaw dish, peppers, and croutons. Preheat oven to 400°. Bake, uncovered, for 20 minutes. Before serving, sprinkle croutons around edge of casserole. Reheat sautéed red and green bell peppers, and mound them in the center. Makes 8 servings.

Summary of processes: Cut ham into cubes; slice 1 red bell pepper and 1 green bell pepper

Freeze in: 13x9x2-inch baking dish; 2 1-quart bags

Serve with: Cooked zucchini, Orange Spiced Tea (page 191)

Note: Great for company that includes children.

HAM AND SWISS PASTRY BAKE

2 cups cooked, cubed ham
1 cup grated Swiss cheese
¼ cup finely chopped celery
¼ cup finely chopped green bell pepper
2 tablespoons minced onion
1 teaspoon dry mustard
1 tablespoon lemon juice
⅓ cup light mayonnaise or salad dressing*
1 9-inch deep-dish, frozen pie shell*

*C*ombine ham, cheese, celery, bell pepper, onion, mustard, and lemon juice in a 1-gallon plastic bag, and store in freezer.

To prepare for serving, thaw ham mixture, add mayonnaise, and put into a 9-inch pie shell. Preheat oven to 375°. Bake, uncovered, for 25 to 35 minutes until golden brown. Serve hot. Makes 6 servings.

Summary of processes: Cut 2 cups ham into cubes; grate 1 cup Swiss cheese; chop ¼ cup celery and ¼ cup bell pepper

Freeze in: 1-gallon bag

Serve with: Frozen Fruit Medley (page 197)

CHAPTER FIVE

STOVE-TOP BARBECUED CHICKEN

1 teaspoon vegetable oil
1 cup finely chopped onion
⅓ cup catsup
⅓ cup water
4 teaspoons white vinegar
4 teaspoons brown sugar
1½ teaspoons Worcestershire sauce
½ teaspoon chili powder
¼ teaspoon crushed celery seed
2 pounds skinless chicken pieces
1 8-ounce package spinach or wide egg noodles*

*H*eat oil in a large, nonstick skillet; sauté onion until tender. Stir in catsup, water, vinegar, brown sugar, Worcestershire sauce, chili powder, and celery seed. Bring sauce to a boil. Add the chicken to the skillet, placing the side down that has the skin removed; spoon sauce over the pieces. Bring to a boil; reduce heat. Cover and simmer 30 minutes. Turn chicken pieces, and simmer covered for about 20 minutes more or until chicken is cooked through. Cool and freeze chicken and sauce.

To prepare for serving, thaw chicken and sauce; put in a large skillet and cook over medium heat, stirring constantly until bubbly. Cook package of spinach or egg noodles according to package directions; serve chicken over noodles. Makes 4 servings.

Summary of processes: Chop 1 cup onion

Freeze in: 4-cup container

Serve with: Corn on the cob, Low-Calorie Chocolate Cake (page 194)

RECIPES

CHICKEN PACKETS

2 cups cooked, chopped chicken
1 3-ounce package cream cheese, softened
1 tablespoon chopped chives
2 tablespoons milk
Salt to taste
½ cup crushed, seasoned crouton crumbs*
2 8-ounce packages refrigerated crescent rolls*
¼ cup (½ stick) melted margarine*

*M*ix chicken, cream cheese, chives, milk, and salt in a medium bowl (mixing with hands works best) to make filling, and store in a 1-quart freezer bag. Put crouton crumbs in another 1-quart bag, attach it to bag of chicken filling, and freeze. Refrigerate crescent rolls.

To prepare for serving, thaw chicken mixture. Preheat oven to 350°. Unroll crescent rolls. Each tube will contain 4 rectangles of dough with a diagonal perforation. Press dough along each perforation so that the rectangle halves will not separate. Place about ¼ cup of chicken mixture into the center of each rectangle. Fold dough over the filling, and pinch the edges to seal tightly. Dip each packet in melted margarine, and coat with crouton crumbs. Place packets on a baking sheet. Bake for 20 minutes or until golden brown. Packets are good either hot or cold. (Serve early in the month before date expires on crescent rolls.) Makes 8 packets.

Summary of processes: Chop 2 cups cooked chicken and 1 tablespoon chives

Freeze in: 2 1-quart bags

Serve with: Smoky Corn Chowder (page 198), baked apples stuffed with plump raisins

Note: These packets are a favorite with children.

WILD RICE CHICKEN

1 6¼-ounce package quick-cooking long grain and wild rice
1 cup cooked, chopped chicken
1 8-ounce can sliced water chestnuts, drained
1 cup finely chopped celery
1¼ cups finely chopped onion
1 cup light mayonnaise*
1 10¾-ounce can condensed cream of mushroom soup*

Cook rice according to package directions. Combine rice with chopped chicken, water chestnuts, celery, and onion; put mixture in a 1-gallon freezer bag.

To prepare for serving, thaw rice and chicken mixture, remove from bag, and place in a 2½-quart baking dish that has been treated with nonstick spray. Preheat oven to 325°. Stir mayonnaise and condensed cream of mushroom soup together and spread over top of chicken. Cover and bake for 1 hour. Makes 6 servings.

Summary of processes: Chop 1 cup cooked chicken, 1 cup celery, and 1¼ cups onion

Freeze in: 1-gallon bag

Serve with: Cooked green beans, peach halves with cottage cheese topped with a maraschino cherry

FRUITY CURRIED CHICKEN

¾ cup regular, uncooked rice
1 cup finely chopped onion
2½ cups chicken broth
1 8¾-ounce can apricots, drained
2¼ cups cooked, chopped chicken
¾ teaspoon salt
¼ teaspoon curry powder
¼ teaspoon pepper
2 teaspoons lemon juice
⅓ cup raisins

*I*n a medium saucepan, heat rice, onion, and chicken broth to a boil, stirring once or twice. Reduce heat to low; cover and simmer 15 minutes. Do not lift lid or stir rice. Drain and cut apricots into pieces. Combine all ingredients. Allow to cool, and store in freezer.

To prepare for serving, thaw and preheat oven to 350°. Put entrée in baking dish treated with nonstick spray and cover with foil. Bake for 1 hour. (Add a small amount of water if it becomes too dry while baking.) Makes 4 servings.

Summary of processes: Chop 1 cup onion and 2¼ cups cooked chicken

Freeze in: 4-cup container

Serve with: Fresh Baked Asparagus (page 200)

HEAVENLY CHICKEN

1 10-ounce package frozen, chopped spinach
½ cup sliced green onion
2 tablespoons margarine
2 tablespoons all-purpose flour
1 cup milk
1 cup soda cracker crumbs
1 cup grated Parmesan cheese
8 boneless chicken breast halves, skinned, about 3¾ pounds
1 cup cooked, cubed ham

*I*n a small saucepan, cook spinach according to package directions; drain well. In a medium saucepan, make white sauce; sauté onion in margarine over low heat until tender. Stir in flour, adding milk all at once. Cook over low heat, stirring constantly until bubbly. Boil and stir 1 minute more until smooth and thickened.

Combine cracker crumbs and cheese. Dip chicken breast halves in crumb mixture to coat lightly. Arrange breast halves in a 13x9x2-inch baking dish that has been treated with nonstick spray. Seal leftover crumb mixture in a 1-quart bag.

Stir spinach and ham into white sauce; spoon sauce over chicken breasts. Allow to cool and cover baking dish with foil, attaching bag of crumb mixture to side of dish.

To prepare for serving, thaw and preheat oven to 350°. Cover and bake for 60 to 75 minutes. Uncover and sprinkle top with crumbs. Bake 10 minutes more. Makes 8 servings.

Summary of processes: Slice ½ cup green onion; crush 1 cup cracker crumbs; cut 1 cup ham into cubes

Freeze in: 13x9x2-inch baking dish; 1-quart bag

Serve with: Pineapple chunks and mandarin oranges sprinkled with shredded coconut, Cranberry Tea (page 191)

Note: This is practically a meal-in-one dish.

CHINESE CHICKEN MORSELS

1 pound boneless, skinless chicken breasts (2 cups)
½ cup lemon juice
¼ cup soy sauce
¼ cup Dijon mustard
2 teaspoons vegetable oil
¼ teaspoon cayenne pepper
1 cup regular, uncooked rice*

*C*ut chicken breasts (kitchen scissors work best) into 1-inch cubes. Mix lemon juice, soy sauce, mustard, oil, and pepper. Put marinade and chicken cubes in a 1-gallon bag, and store in the freezer.

To prepare for serving, thaw chicken and remove from marinade. Preheat oven to broil and/or 550°. Warm marinade in a small saucepan. Place cubes about an inch apart on broiler pan treated with nonstick spray. Broil 4 to 5 inches from heat for 7 minutes, brushing with marinade once. Turn chicken cubes, and broil another 4 minutes. Meanwhile, prepare rice according to package directions. Heat remaining marinade and serve over rice. Makes 4 to 5 servings.

Summary of processes: Cut chicken into 1-inch cubes

Freeze in: 1-gallon bag

Serve with: Sliced, fresh tomatoes or tossed salad, Banana-Applesauce Muffins (page 185)

Note: For a luncheon alternative, toss sautéed or broiled chicken morsels with mixed salad greens, shredded carrots, cherry tomatoes, chopped green bell pepper, sliced water chestnuts, and croutons. Use your favorite low-calorie dressing.

POULET DE FRANCE

1 12-ounce package seasoned bread stuffing—7-pound bird size (6 cups)
2 tablespoons melted margarine
2 cups chicken broth, divided
3 cups cooked, chopped chicken
½ cup finely chopped onion
¼ cup minced chives
½ cup finely chopped celery
½ cup light mayonnaise
¾ teaspoon salt
2 eggs
1½ cups milk
1 10¾-ounce can condensed cream of mushroom soup
½ cup grated mild cheddar cheese

*I*n a medium bowl, mix stuffing, melted margarine, and 1¼ cups broth. Mix chicken, ¾ cup broth, onions, chives, celery, mayonnaise, and salt in another bowl. Spread half the stuffing in a 13x9x2-inch baking dish treated with nonstick spray. Spread chicken mixture over stuffing. Cover with remaining stuffing. Whisk eggs, milk, and soup in a large bowl. Pour sauce evenly over stuffing. Cover dish with foil and freeze. Put cheese in a small freezer bag and attach it to dish.

To prepare for serving, thaw grated cheese and chicken. Preheat oven to 325°. Cover and bake for 30 minutes. Remove foil, sprinkle with cheese, and continue to bake uncovered for 10 minutes more. Makes 8 servings.

Summary of processes: Chop 3 cups cooked chicken, ½ cup onion, and ½ cup celery; mince ¼ cup chives; grate ½ cup mild cheddar cheese

Freeze in: 13x9x2-inch baking dish; 1-quart bag

Serve with: Cooked frozen peas, Cranberry Sauce

MEAL-IN-ONE POTATOES

½ **pound freshly ground turkey**
½ **cup finely chopped onion**
1 **teaspoon minced garlic (1 clove)**
1 **cup canned, red kidney beans, drained**
1 **8-ounce can tomato sauce**
½ **cup chili sauce**
1 **teaspoon dried oregano leaves**
¼ **teaspoon salt**
4 **medium baking potatoes***

*I*n a medium skillet, cook ground turkey, onion, and garlic until turkey is browned; add remaining ingredients except potatoes. Bring to a boil; reduce heat. Simmer 5 minutes. Cool and freeze in a 1-quart bag.

To serve, thaw filling. Preheat oven to 400°. Prepare and bake potatoes for 1 hour or until done. Heat filling until bubbly. Split tops of baked potatoes lengthwise, and fluff pulp with a fork. Top each potato with filling. Makes 4 servings.

Summary of processes: Chop ½ cup onion; mince 1 clove garlic

Freeze in: 1-quart bag

Serve with: Smoky Corn Chowder (page 198)

TERIYAKI CHICKEN

½ cup soy sauce
½ cup sugar
1½ tablespoons red wine vinegar
2 teaspoons vegetable oil
1 small garlic clove, minced
¾ teaspoon ground ginger
1 pound boneless, skinless chicken breasts
1 cup regular, uncooked rice*

*M*ix soy sauce, sugar, vinegar, oil, garlic, and ginger to make marinade (reserve 2 tablespoons in a small bowl for Teriyaki Burgers). Freeze chicken in marinade in a 1-gallon bag.

When preparing to serve, thaw chicken. Preheat oven to 350°. Pour chicken and marinade into a baking dish that has been coated with nonstick spray. Bake for 35 minutes. Prepare rice according to package directions. Serve chicken over rice. Makes 4 servings.

Summary of processes: Mince 1 clove garlic

Freeze in: 1-gallon bag

Serve with: Cooked French-cut green beans

RECIPES

MIMI'S CHICKEN SOUP

1 small onion
2 or 3 whole cloves
1 cup chopped, cooked chicken
2 quarts chicken broth
½ teaspoon salt
1 tablespoon chopped fresh parsley
3 shredded carrots
½ cup sliced celery with leaves
1 8-ounce package (use half) tortellini*

*P*eel and cut ends off onion; insert whole cloves into the onion. In a large pot, combine onion, chicken, broth, salt, parsley, carrots, and celery. Bring to a boil; reduce heat. Simmer uncovered for 1½ hours. Remove onion. Cool soup, put in container, and store in freezer.

To prepare for serving, thaw soup, put in large pot, and heat until bubbly. Add half a package tortellini, and boil 25 minutes more. Makes 4 servings.

Summary of processes: Chop cooked chicken; shred 3 carrots; slice ½ cup celery; chop 1 tablespoon parsley

Freeze in: 8-cup container

Serve with: Swedish Rye Bread (page 184)

BAKED HERB FISH FILLETS

4 fish fillets (about 1¼ pounds orange roughy or sole)*
½ cup Italian-flavored bread crumbs
¼ cup grated Parmesan cheese
¼ teaspoon garlic powder
¼ teaspoon salt
1 egg white, lightly beaten*
4 to 5 new potatoes*
1 small lemon*

*F*reeze fish fillets in a 1-gallon bag. Combine bread crumbs, Parmesan cheese, garlic powder, and salt in a 1-quart bag; attach to fish fillet package.

To prepare to serve, thaw fish and herbs. Preheat oven to 375°. Lightly beat egg white, and dip fillets in it. Put fillets one at a time in bag with herb mixture; make sure each is coated. Remove and arrange fillets in baking dish that has been treated with nonstick spray. Bake for about 15 minutes (until fish flakes easily) or in microwave oven on high for 4 to 5 minutes.

At the same time, prepare new potatoes. Peel a strip around the center of each potato. Heat 1 cup salted water to a boil; add potatoes. Cover, heat till boiling; reduce heat. Simmer, tightly covered, until tender, 30 to 35 minutes; drain. Serve potatoes with fish and lemon wedges. Makes 4 servings.

Freeze in: 1-gallon and 1-quart bag

Serve with: Cooked zucchini

RECIPES

AZTEC QUICHE

1¼ cups grated Monterey Jack cheese
¾ cup grated mild cheddar cheese
1 9-inch deep-dish frozen pie shell
1 4-ounce can diced green chilies
1 cup half-and-half
3 eggs, lightly beaten
½ teaspoon salt
⅛ teaspoon ground cumin

*S*pread Monterey Jack cheese and half of cheddar cheese over bottom of pie shell. Sprinkle diced chilies over cheeses. Stir together in a bowl the half-and-half, eggs, and seasonings. Pour carefully into pie shell. Sprinkle with remaining cheddar. Cover pie with foil, and put in freezer.

To prepare for serving, thaw pie and remove foil. Preheat oven to 325°. Bake, uncovered, for 40 to 50 minutes. Makes 6 to 8 servings.

Summary of processes: Grate 1¼ cups Monterey Jack cheese and ¾ cup mild cheddar cheese

Freeze in: 9-inch oven-proof quiche or pie pan

Serve with: Fresh fruit salad, Cinnamon Logs (page 187)

CHAPTER FIVE

BAKED EGGS

6 bread slices, cut in cubes
2 cups grated mild cheddar cheese
1 cup cooked, cubed ham
¼ cup finely chopped green bell pepper
½ cup finely chopped onion
6 eggs
3 cups milk

*M*ix bread, cheese, ham, bell pepper, and onion; spread in a 13x9x2-inch baking dish treated with nonstick spray. Whisk eggs and milk and pour over top. Cover dish with foil and freeze.

To prepare for serving, thaw dish and preheat oven to 375°. Bake, uncovered, for 45 minutes. Makes 8 to 10 servings.

Summary of processes: Cut bread and ham into cubes; grate 2 cups mild cheddar cheese; chop ¼ cup green bell pepper and ½ cup onion

Freeze in: 13x9x2-inch baking dish

Serve with: Frozen Fruit Medley (page 197)

Note: This dish is good with 6 slices cooked, crumbled bacon instead of ham. You can also make this dish the night before, refrigerate it, and bake and serve it the next morning. It's nice for company brunch after church.

RECIPES

TERIYAKI BURGERS

1 pound lean ground beef
2 tablespoons teriyaki sauce (see recipe for Teriyaki Chicken
    marinade)
4 sandwich rolls*

*M*ix teriyaki sauce into ground beef; form four patties. Freeze patties in a 1-gallon freezer bag with a piece of waxed paper between each patty. Freeze sandwich rolls.

To serve, thaw rolls and patties. Grill or fry meat to desired pinkness. Serve on warmed sandwich rolls. Makes 4 servings.

Freeze in: 1-gallon bag

Serve with: Potato salad, pickles, and ripe olives

CHAPTER FIVE

BACON-WRAPPED BURGERS

4 strips bacon
1 pound lean ground beef
Salt to taste
Lemon pepper
¼ cup grated Parmesan cheese
1 2-ounce can mushroom stems and pieces, drained
1 tablespoon minced onion
2 tablespoons finely chopped green bell pepper

*I*n a small skillet or microwave, cook bacon until limp. Drain bacon on paper towel. Pat ground beef on waxed paper into a 12x8x¼-inch rectangle. Sprinkle lightly with salt and lemon pepper. Top with Parmesan cheese.

Combine mushrooms, onion, and bell pepper; sprinkle evenly over ground beef. Roll ground beef like a jelly roll, starting from the longest side. Cut into four slices. Wrap edge of each slice with a strip of partially cooked bacon, securing with wooden picks. Freeze hamburgers with a piece of waxed paper between each patty.

To serve, thaw patties; grill over medium coals 8 minutes. Turn and grill 8 more minutes or to desired doneness; or broil hamburgers. Makes 4 servings.

Summary of processes: Chop 2 tablespoons green bell pepper

Freeze in: 1-gallon bag

Serve with: Twice-Baked Potatoes Deluxe (page 200), Marinated Veggies (page 201)

RECIPES

RAVIOLI SOUP

1 pound lean ground beef (2½ cups browned meat)
¼ cup soft bread crumbs
¼ cup grated Parmesan cheese
¾ teaspoon onion salt
2 teaspoons minced garlic (2 cloves)
1 tablespoon olive oil or vegetable oil
1½ cups finely chopped onion
1 28-ounce can Italian-style or plain crushed tomatoes in puree
1 6-ounce can tomato paste
1 14½-ounce can beef broth or bouillon
1 cup water
½ teaspoon sugar
½ teaspoon dried basil leaves
¼ teaspoon dried thyme leaves
¼ teaspoon dried oregano leaves
¼ cup chopped fresh parsley
1 12-ounce package plain ravioli without sauce* (located in the
    frozen or refrigerated section)
Grated Parmesan cheese*

*B*rown the ground beef in a large pot; combine remaining ingredients except frozen ravioli and additional Parmesan cheese. Bring soup to a boil; reduce heat. Cover and simmer 10 minutes, stirring occasionally. Cool, put in container, and freeze.

    To prepare for serving, thaw soup base and put in a large pot. Bring to a boil; reduce heat. Simmer, uncovered, for at least 30 minutes, stirring occasionally. Thaw and cook ravioli according to package directions until just tender. Drain ravioli; add to soup. Salt to taste. Serve with Parmesan cheese. Makes 6 servings.

Summary of processes: Mince 2 cloves garlic; chop 1¾ cup onion and ¼ cup parsley

Freeze in: 8-cup container

Serve with: Tossed green salad, Dawn's French Bread (page 183)

MANICOTTI

1 8-ounce package manicotti
1 tablespoon vegetable oil
1 15-ounce carton part-skim ricotta cheese
1 16-ounce carton small curd, low-fat cottage cheese
1 cup grated mozzarella cheese
⅓ cup grated Parmesan cheese
1 teaspoon salt
¼ teaspoon pepper
1 tablespoon chopped fresh parsley
2 eggs
2½ cups Spaghetti Sauce

*B*oil manicotti according to package directions, adding oil to water so they won't stick together. Meanwhile, mix ricotta cheese, cottage cheese, mozzarella and Parmesan cheeses, salt, pepper, parsley, and eggs.

Drain manicotti; run cold water over it. Stuff each manicotti with cheese mixture. Place them in a 3-quart casserole after treating the dish with nonstick spray, and pour sauce around stuffed manicotti. Cover dish with foil and freeze.

To prepare for serving, thaw and preheat oven to 350°. Cover and bake for 45 minutes. Uncover and bake for 15 minutes more. Makes 8 servings.

Summary of processes: Grate 1 cup mozzarella cheese; chop 1 tablespoon parsley

Freeze in: 3-quart casserole

Serve with: Spinach salad

TACO PIE

1½ pounds lean ground beef (3¾ cups browned)
⅓ cup finely chopped onion (¼ cup sautéed)
1 1¼-ounce package taco seasoning mix
1 4-ounce can diced green chilies, drained
1 cup milk
1 cup biscuit baking mix
2 eggs
2 tomatoes, sliced*
1 cup grated mild cheddar cheese
1 8-ounce carton sour cream*
1 chopped tomato*
Shredded lettuce (enough to garnish pie)*

*I*n a large skillet, cook and stir ground beef and onion until beef is brown; drain. Combine beef with taco seasoning mix, and spread in a 10-inch pie plate treated with nonstick cooking spray. Sprinkle with chilies. Beat milk, baking mix, and eggs until smooth, 15 seconds on high in a blender or 1 minute with hand beater. Pour milk mixture over beef in pie plate. Cover plate with foil and freeze. Freeze 1-quart bag of grated cheese with pie, taped to pie plate.

To prepare for serving, thaw pie and preheat oven to 400°. Bake, uncovered, for 35 minutes. Top with sliced tomatoes; sprinkle with cheese. Bake until golden brown, 8 to 10 minutes. Top with sour cream, chopped tomato, and shredded lettuce. Makes 6 to 8 servings.

Summary of processes: Chop ⅓ cup onion; grate 1 cup cheddar cheese

Freeze in: 10-inch quiche or pie plate; 1-quart bag

Serve with: Guacamole dip with tortilla chips, fruit salad

JOES TO GO

1 pound lean ground beef (2½ cups browned)
¾ cup finely chopped onion (½ cup sautéed)
1½ teaspoons garlic salt
⅛ teaspoon pepper
½ cup chili sauce
¼ cup brown sugar
1 tablespoon white vinegar
1 tablespoon prepared mustard
1 8-ounce can tomato sauce
6 hamburger buns*

*I*n a large skillet, cook and stir ground beef and onion until beef is brown; drain. Add garlic salt, pepper, chili sauce, brown sugar, white vinegar, mustard, and tomato sauce. Bring to a boil; reduce heat. Simmer, uncovered, for 10 minutes, stirring occasionally. Cool and freeze. Keep with hamburger buns.

To prepare for serving, thaw hamburger sauce and buns. Heat sauce until bubbly and serve on warmed buns. Makes enough for 6 buns.

Summary of processes: Chop 1½ cups onion

Freeze in: 8-cup container

Serve with: Potato chips, carrot and celery sticks

WINTER BARLEY

1 pound lean ground beef
¼ cup chopped celery
½ cup chopped onion
¼ cup chopped green bell pepper
1¼ teaspoons salt
½ teaspoon marjoram
1 teaspoon Worcestershire sauce
⅛ teaspoon pepper
1 15-ounce can chopped tomatoes
¾ cup quick-cooking barley

*I*n a large saucepan, sauté the beef, celery, onions, and green pepper until the beef is browned. Add remaining ingredients; label and freeze.

When preparing to serve, thaw and add 1½ cups water. Simmer, covered, for 30 minutes or until barley is tender. Makes 6 servings.

Summary of processes: Chop ¼ cup celery, ½ cup onion, and ¼ cup green pepper

Freeze in: 1-gallon bag

Serve with: Cheesy-Herb Bread (page 180), pear halves with cottage cheese on top

CHAPTER FIVE

CHEESY CORN CASSEROLE

1½ pounds lean ground beef (3¾ cups browned)
1 17-ounce can whole kernel corn, drained
2 eggs, slightly beaten
1 cup small curd cottage cheese with chives, drained
1 tablespoon all-purpose flour
1 8-ounce can tomato sauce
½ teaspoon minced garlic (½ clove)
¼ teaspoon ground cinnamon
1 cup grated mozzarella cheese*

*I*n a large skillet, cook and stir ground beef until brown; drain. Meanwhile, spread corn in bottom of an 8x8x2-inch baking dish sprayed with nonstick spray. Combine eggs and cottage cheese; spread mixture over corn.

Stir flour into browned ground beef; cook 1 minute, stirring constantly. Add tomato sauce, garlic, and cinnamon to meat mixture, and stir together. Layer meat mixture on top of cottage cheese and eggs. Cover dish with foil and put in freezer. Put mozzarella in 1-quart freezer bag; tape to baking dish.

To prepare for serving, thaw meat and cheese and preheat oven to 350°. Sprinkle cheese on top. Bake, uncovered, for 30 minutes. Makes 6 servings.

Summary of processes: Mince ½ teaspoon garlic; grate 1 cup mozzarella cheese

Freeze in: 8x8x2-inch baking dish; 1-quart bag

Serve with: Beets, Spicy Pumpkin Muffins (page 188)

RECIPES

HAM DINNER SLICES

2 ¾-inch-thick cooked ham slices (from center of ham)*
4 medium baking potatoes*
Prepared mustard*
Brown sugar*
About 1 cup milk*

*F*reeze ham slices in 1-gallon bag.

To serve, thaw ham slices. Preheat oven to 400°. Prepare potatoes and bake for about 1 hour or until done. Place ham slices in a single layer in the bottom of an 8x8x2-inch baking dish treated with nonstick spray. Spread mustard on top of each slice; sprinkle brown sugar over mustard. Pour enough milk over ham slices to come halfway up their sides. Bake, uncovered, for 45 minutes. Makes 4 servings.

Freeze in: 1-gallon bag

Serve with: Cooked green beans, Orange Spiced Tea (page 191)

CHAPTER FIVE

CHAPTER SIX
One-Month Entrée Plan B

*A*bigail lost no time. She
took two hundred loaves of
bread, two skins of wine, five
dressed sheep, five seahs of
roasted grain, a hundred cakes
of raisins and two hundred cakes
of pressed figs, and
loaded them on donkeys.

1 Samuel 25:18

Menu

· CALENDAR ·

Sunday	Monday	Tuesday	Wednesday	Thursday	Friday	Saturday
	Eat Out Cooking Day! *1*	Split Pea Soup *2*	Salad Bowl Puff *3*	Jack Burgers *4*	Deborah's Sweet and Sour Chicken *5*	French Stew *6*
Shish Kebabs *7*	Chicken and Rice Pilaf *8*	Grandma's Chili *9*	Crustless Spinach Quiche *10*	Grilled Ham Slices *11*	Green Chili Enchiladas *12*	Chicken à la King *13*
Sausage and Rice *14*	Oriental Chicken *15*	Marinated Flank Steak *16*	Saucy Hot Dogs *17*	Sicilian Meat Roll *18*	Lasagna *19*	Oven Barbecued Chicken and Cheesy Biscuits *20*
Chicken Broccoli *21*	Balkan Meatballs *22*	Baked Beans and Hamburger *23*	Jan's Sandwiches *24*	Bird's Nest Pie *25*	Chicken Tetrazzini *26*	French Dip *27*
Lemon Chicken *28*	Grilled Fish *29*	Mexican Stroganoff *30*				

CHAPTER SIX

GROCERY SHOPPING AND STAPLES LISTS

An asterisk (*) after an item indicates that it should be stored until the day you serve the dish that calls for it. Mark those items as a reminder that you will need them for an entrée.

When entrées require perishable foods to be refrigerated until served, you may want to prepare those dishes right away or buy the food the week you plan to make the dish. For example, fresh mushrooms would spoil by the end of a month.

For one-month entrée plan B, you will need these food items as well as the ones in the staples list that follows:

GROCERY SHOPPING LIST

Canned Goods

1 bottle barbecue sauce (1 cup, your favorite)*
1 10¾-ounce can beef consommé
1 8-ounce bottle chili sauce
2 10¾-ounce cans condensed cream of chicken soup
4 10¾-ounce cans condensed cream of mushroom soup
1 4-ounce can diced green chilies
1 4-ounce can green chili salsa
1 16-ounce can whole green beans
1 15-ounce can kidney beans
1 24-ounce bottle red wine vinegar (about 2 cups)
1 8-ounce, 3 4-ounce, and 1 2-ounce cans mushroom stems and pieces
1 2-ounce jar pimientos
1 31-ounce can pork and beans
2 8-ounce cans pineapple chunks (1*)
1 17-ounce bottle soy sauce (about 1⅛ cups)
3 16-ounce cans peeled tomatoes
1 12-ounce and 2 6-ounce cans tomato paste
1 15-ounce and 1 8-ounce cans tomato sauce
1 small can tomato juice
2 8-ounce cans sliced water chestnuts

Grains, Pasta, and Rice

1 12-ounce package Hungry Jack buttermilk biscuits*

½ cup fine, dry bread crumbs

6 hot dog buns*

16 sandwich or onion rolls (8*)

4 hamburger buns*

1 8-ounce package lasagna

1 5-ounce can chow mein noodles*

1 12-ounce and 1 8-ounce package wide egg noodles*

12 ounces dry, green split peas

1 32-ounce and 1 16-ounce package regular rice

1 16-ounce package spaghetti

8 to 12 flour tortillas

1 6¼-ounce package fast-cooking long grain and wild rice (use Uncle Ben's if available)

⅓ cup crushed, seasoned croutons

Dry Ingredients and Seasonings

1 1½-ounce package onion soup mix

1 1-ounce package French's or Good Seasons French dip or brown gravy mix*

Frozen Foods

1¼ pounds frozen fish fillets (halibut, swordfish, or orange roughy)*

1 10-ounce package chopped broccoli

1 10-ounce package peas (use half)

1 10-ounce package chopped spinach

1 10-ounce package puff pastry shells* (6 shells)

2 10-ounce packages frozen peas and pearl onions

Dairy Products

¾ cup (1½ sticks) margarine or butter

13 eggs (2*)

1 16-ounce carton small curd, low-fat cottage cheese

2 12-ounce cartons large curd, low-fat cottage cheese

4 8-ounce cartons sour cream (or 1 carton 8-ounce low-fat yogurt for one of the cartons
    of sour cream)

1 8-ounce jar Cheez Whiz

12 ounces (3 cups) grated mild cheddar cheese

26 ounces Monterey Jack cheese (4 thin slices, 6 cups grated)

16 ounces sliced mozzarella cheese; 8 ounces grated mozzarella cheese

7 ounces (about 1¾ cups) grated Parmesan cheese

1 cup half-and-half

1 quart milk

Meat and Poultry

2 pounds boneless, cubed, top sirloin steak

10 pounds lean ground beef (or turkey)

1⅓ pounds flank steak

2 pounds round steak

3 to 4 pounds sirloin tip or boneless beef rump roast

3 pounds beef stew meat

12½ pounds whole chicken or 10 pounds chicken breasts

4 boneless, skinless chicken breasts

3½ pounds chicken pieces (breasts, thighs, or drumsticks)

4 strips bacon

4 pounds cooked ham (1½ pounds cubed, ½ pound sliced thin, and 2 pounds from the
    center portion cut in 2 ¾-inch-thick dinner slices*)

½ pound ground turkey

2 pounds bulk Italian or turkey sausage

6 hot dogs or turkey franks*

1 2½-ounce package thin-sliced, corned beef luncheon meat

Produce

4 carrots

1 bunch celery

8 teaspoons minced garlic (8 cloves)

1 bunch green onions

5 green bell peppers (4¼ cups chopped, ½ to store*)

4 ounces whole fresh mushrooms*

4¼ pounds yellow onions

5 to 6 new potatoes

Half-pint box cherry tomatoes*

1 small bunch fresh parsley

STAPLES LIST

Make sure you have the following staples on hand; add those you don't have to the above shopping list:

ground allspice

dried basil leaves

bay leaves

biscuit baking mix (½ cup)

soft bread crumbs (1 slice)

brown sugar (1⅛ cups)

catsup (¼ cup)

chicken bouillon cube

chili powder

ground cinnamon

cornstarch

curry powder

all-purpose flour (about ¾ cup)

garlic powder

ground ginger

lemon juice (⅓ cup)

light mayonnaise (about 1 cup)

minced onion

minute tapioca (¼ cup)

nonstick spray

ground nutmeg

olive oil

onion powder

onion salt

dried oregano leaves

paprika

parsley flakes

pepper

prepared mustard

salt

seasoned salt

sugar (½ cup plus ¾ teaspoon)

dried thyme leaves

vegetable oil (about ¾ cup)

white vinegar (½ cup)

Worcestershire sauce

FREEZER CONTAINERS

The following list of freezer containers or baking dishes will be needed for the entrées. These are not the only containers you could use, but this list gives you an idea of the size and number of containers you'll need.

Heavy aluminum foil:
Jan's Sandwiches

5 1-quart freezer bags:
Green Chili Enchiladas, Bird's Nest Pie, Grilled Fish, Crustless Spinach Quiche, Oven Barbecued Chicken and Cheesy Biscuits

12 1-gallon freezer bags:
Grilled Ham Slices, Balkan Meatballs, Jack Burgers, Sausage and Rice, Lemon Chicken, Chicken à la King, Oriental Chicken, Salad Bowl Puff, Marinated Flank Steak, Oven Barbecued Chicken and Cheesy Biscuits, Sicilian Meat Roll

1 2-cup container:
Grandma's Chili for Saucy Hot Dogs

1 5-cup container:
Baked Beans and Hamburger

6 6-cup containers:
Split Pea Soup, Grandma's Chili, Chicken Tetrazzini (2), Shish Kebabs, Mexican Stroganoff

1 8-cup container:
Deborah's Sweet and Sour Chicken

1 14-cup container:
French Stew

1 11x7x1½-inch baking dish:
Chicken and Rice Pilaf

3 13x9x2-inch baking dishes:
Lasagna, Green Chili Enchiladas, Chicken Broccoli

2 10-inch quiche or pie plates:
Bird's Nest Pie, Crustless Spinach Quiche

THE DAY BEFORE COOKING DAY

1. Freeze hamburger buns, hot dog buns, puff pastry shells, frozen fish fillets, ham dinner slices, and all but 8 of the sandwich rolls.

2. Refrigerate ½ green bell pepper, whole fresh mushrooms, 1 whole onion, and cherry tomatoes for Shish Kebabs.

3. Refrigerate 7½ pounds lean ground beef, sirloin tip or beef rump roast, 4 boneless chicken breasts, and 1 pound chicken pieces. Freeze remaining 2½ pounds chicken pieces for Oven Barbecued Chicken and Cheesy Biscuits in a 1-gallon bag marked with name of recipe.

4. Cover remaining whole chickens or breasts with at least 9 cups water in a large pot. Bring to a boil; reduce heat. Cover and simmer until thickest pieces are done, about 45 minutes to 1 hour. Cool chicken until ready to handle. Remove meat from bones and skin. Cut chicken into bite-size pieces with kitchen scissors, which are easier to use than a knife. Refrigerate chicken pieces in two plastic bags. (You will need 15½ cups chopped, cooked chicken.)

5. Refrigerate 3 cups chicken broth; discard remaining broth or use for soup.

6. Set out appliances, bowls, canned goods, dry ingredients, freezer containers, and recipes.

7. Rinse split peas, and soak them covered with cold water overnight.

8. Start French Stew in Crockpot (just before bed).

COOKING DAY ASSEMBLY ORDER

Make sure you've cleared the table and counters of unnecessary kitchenware to allow plenty of working room. It also helps to have fresh, damp washcloths and towels for wiping your hands and the cooking area. The day will go a lot smoother if you clean and organize as you work.

Before you prepare a recipe, gather all the spices and ingredients in the assembly area to save time and steps. When you finish the recipe, remove unneeded items, and wipe off the work space.

BEFORE ASSEMBLING DISHES

1. Cool and freeze French Stew. Wash out Crockpot.

2. Perform all chopping, crushing, grating, and slicing tasks.

> Bacon: dice ¼ pound and 3 strips (put in separate dishes).
> Ham: dice 2 cups; slice ½ pound thin; make thick dinner slices from the rest.
> Round steak: cut into bite-size pieces.
> Onions: chop 11⅔ cups fine; cut up 1¾ cups coarsely for Shish Kebabs and Deborah's Sweet and Sour Chicken.
> Green onions: chop onion bulbs only; discard green tops.
> Green bell peppers: chop 3¼ cups; cut 1 cup in coarse pieces for Deborah's Sweet and Sour Chicken; save half of pepper for Shish Kebabs.
> Celery: chop 1⅓ cups fine and 1 cup in coarse pieces; put in separate containers.
> Carrots: peel and slice ¾ cup and 3 large; put in separate containers.
> Garlic: mince 7 cloves (7 teaspoons).
> Mozzarella cheese: slice all.
> Mild cheddar cheese: grate all.
> Monterey Jack cheese: cut 4 thin slices; grate remaining cheese.
> Crumbs: crush ½ cup fine, dry bread crumbs; ¼ cup crouton crumbs; ¾ cup soft bread crumbs.

3. Put ½ cup grated mild cheddar cheese in a 1-quart freezer bag; tape it to bag of chicken pieces for Oven Barbecued Chicken and Cheesy Biscuits.

4. Cook and stir 5¼ pounds ground beef in a large skillet until brown.

5. In another large skillet, sauté 8½ cups onions in margarine until tender.

6. Spray pans or baking dishes you will need with nonstick spray (check list of freezer containers on pages 137–138).

7. Skim and discard fat from chicken broth.

8. Drain browned ground beef and sautéed onions; set them aside.

ASSEMBLE BEEF DISHES

1. Assemble Grandma's Chili in Crockpot using 5 cups browned ground beef and ¾ cup sautéed onions.

2. Start baking sirloin tip or boneless beef rump roast for French Dip.

3. Make Lasagna using 2½ cups browned ground beef.

4. Start Mexican Stroganoff simmering in a large saucepan.

5. Assemble Baked Beans and Hamburger using 2 cups browned ground beef and ½ cup sautéed onions.

6. Prepare Balkan Meatballs.

7. Prepare Sicilian Meat Roll.

8. While meatballs are broiling, assemble Green Chili Enchiladas using 3¾ cups browned ground beef and ¾ cup sautéed onions.

9. Make Jack Burgers.

10. Freeze beef dishes.

ASSEMBLE SAUSAGE DISHES

1. Brown 2 pounds of Italian or turkey sausage; drain.

2. Break 1-pound package spaghetti in half and cook as directed on package until al dente; drain. Toss half the noodles in ½ tablespoon oil to prevent noodles from sticking together; set aside for Chicken Tetrazzini.

3. Assemble Bird's Nest Pie, using remaining half of noodles.

4. Prepare Sausage and Rice.

5. Freeze sausage dishes.

ASSEMBLE CHICKEN DISHES

1. Complete Chicken Tetrazzini.

2. Prepare Deborah's Sweet and Sour Chicken.

3. Make Lemon Chicken.

4. Complete Chicken à la King.

5. Assemble Chicken Broccoli.

6. Prepare Chicken and Rice Pilaf.

7. Make Oriental Chicken.

8. Freeze chicken dishes.

ASSEMBLE HAM DISHES

1. Start Split Pea Soup simmering.

2. Assemble Salad Bowl Puff.

3. Complete Currant Ham Loaf.

4. Freeze ham dishes.

ASSEMBLE MISCELLANEOUS DISHES

1. Assemble marinade for Grilled Fish.

2. Complete Marinated Flank Steak.

3. Prepare Shish Kebabs.

4. Complete Crustless Spinach Quiche.

5. Make Jan's Sandwiches.

6. Cool and freeze Grandma's Chili and Split Pea Soup.

7. Cool and slice sirloin tip or boneless beef rump roast for French Dip.

8. Freeze miscellaneous dishes.

RECIPES FOR ONE-MONTH ENTRÉE PLAN B

Each recipe offers complete instructions on how to prepare the dish. Food items with an asterisk (*) won't be prepared until you serve the entrée. For recipes calling for oven baking, preheat oven for about 10 minutes.

"Summary of processes" gives a quick overview of foods that need to be chopped, diced, grated, or sliced. "Freeze in" tells what bags and containers will be needed to freeze each entrée. "Serve with" offers suggestions of foods to accompany the meal. Some of the recipes for those foods are included in chapter 8; page numbers are indicated for easy reference. "Note" includes special instructions on how the entrée can be used in other ways.

FRENCH STEW

3 pounds beef stew meat
1 10¾-ounce can beef consommé
3 large peeled and sliced carrots
1 16-ounce can whole green beans, drained
2 10-ounce packages frozen peas and pearl onions
1 16-ounce can peeled tomatoes
1 cup water
⅓ cup red wine vinegar
¼ cup minute tapioca
1 tablespoon brown sugar
½ cup fine, dry bread crumbs
1 bay leaf
1 tablespoon salt
¼ teaspoon pepper

*P*reheat oven to 250°. Mix ingredients in a large, covered pot, breaking apart the frozen peas and onions. Bake for 6 to 8 hours, or cook in a large Crockpot 8 to 10 hours on low. Allow to cool, and put in freezer container.

To prepare for serving, thaw stew and heat until bubbly in a large pot. Makes 8 servings.

Summary of processes: Peel and slice 3 large carrots

Freeze in: 14-cup container

Serve with: Frozen Fruit Medley (page 197), Dawn's French Bread (page 183)

Note: This stew can be served over cooked wild rice. If you prefer potatoes, cook them and then add to stew when you serve it. (Note that potatoes don't freeze well.) You could also serve this stew on cooking day, freezing what's left over to serve later.

GRANDMA'S CHILI

2 pounds lean ground beef (5 cups browned)
1½ cups finely chopped onion (¾ cup sautéed)
1 cup chopped green bell pepper
1 tablespoon Worcestershire sauce
¾ teaspoon chili powder
¼ teaspoon ground cinnamon
⅛ teaspoon garlic powder
Salt and black pepper to taste
1 15-ounce can kidney beans, drained
1 16-ounce can peeled tomatoes
1 6-ounce can tomato paste
1 15-ounce can tomato sauce

*B*rown ground beef with onion in a large saucepan; add remaining ingredients. Bring to a boil; reduce heat. Cover and simmer over low heat for 2 hours on a back burner, or cook in a Crockpot on low for 6 hours, stirring occasionally. Cool, freeze in 1 6-cup container and 1 2-cup container for Saucy Hot Dogs.

To serve chili, thaw and heat in saucepan until hot and bubbly. Makes 12 servings.

Summary of Processes: Chop 1½ cups onion and 1 cup green bell pepper

Freeze in: 6-cup container, Grandma's Chili; 2-cup container, Saucy Hot Dogs

Serve with: Cornbread, cottage cheese with pineapple chunks and mandarin orange slices

Note: This is a nice warm-up meal on a chilly day.

FRENCH DIP

3 to 4 pounds sirloin tip or boneless beef rump roast
Worcestershire sauce
8 sandwich rolls*
1 packet French's or Good Seasons French dip or brown gravy mix*

*P*lace roast in roasting pan on a piece of heavy aluminum foil large enough to wrap meat in. Douse roast with Worcestershire sauce; seal meat in foil. Bake in preheated oven at 350° for 4 to 5 hours on middle rack.

Remove roast from oven; allow it to sit twenty minutes before slicing. Save meat juices and put in a 1-gallon bag with sliced meat.

To serve, thaw sandwich rolls, roast, and juices. Pour juices into a saucepan; add seasoning packet. Bring to a boil, reduce heat, and simmer according to package directions. Warm sandwich rolls and meat in a small amount of juice. Serve thin slices of roast in sandwich rolls with bowls of juice for dipping. Makes 6 to 8 servings.

Freeze in: 1-gallon bag

Serve with: Waldorf salad, carrot strips

RECIPES

LASAGNA

1 pound lean ground beef (2½ cups browned)
1 teaspoon minced garlic (1 clove)
1 tablespoon parsley flakes
1 tablespoon dried basil leaves
1½ teaspoons salt
1 16-ounce can peeled tomatoes
1 12-ounce can tomato paste
1 8-ounce package lasagna
2 12-ounce cartons large curd, low-fat cottage cheese
2 eggs, beaten
½ teaspoon pepper
2 tablespoons parsley flakes
½ cup grated Parmesan cheese
12 ounces sliced mozzarella cheese

*I*n a large saucepan, mix browned ground beef, garlic, parsley, basil, salt, tomatoes, and tomato paste. Bring to a boil; reduce heat. Simmer, uncovered, for 30 minutes, stirring frequently.

Cook noodles according to package directions until al dente; drain. Combine cottage cheese, eggs, pepper, parsley flakes, and Parmesan cheese. Grease a 13x9x2-inch baking dish. Place a layer of noodles in dish, spread half the cottage cheese mixture over noodles, layer with half the mozzarella, top with half the sauce mixture. Repeat process, topping with noodles and covering with sauce. Wrap dish with foil and freeze.

To prepare for serving, thaw lasagna and preheat oven to 375°. Bake, uncovered, for 30 to 40 minutes. Makes 8 servings.

Summary of processes: Mince 1 clove garlic; slice 12 ounces mozzarella cheese

Freeze in: 13x9x2-inch baking dish

Serve with: Tossed green salad

Note: Invite youth group members or harried youth group workers over for Lasagna.

MEXICAN STROGANOFF

2 pounds round steak
1 cup finely chopped onion
2 teaspoons minced garlic (2 cloves)
2 tablespoons vegetable oil
⅓ cup red wine vinegar
1¾ cups water
½ cup chili sauce
1 tablespoon paprika
1 tablespoon chili powder
2 teaspoons seasoned salt
1 teaspoon soy sauce
1 8-ounce can mushroom stems and pieces, drained
1 8-ounce carton (1 cup) sour cream or low-fat yogurt*
3 tablespoons all-purpose flour*
1 12-ounce package wide egg noodles*

*C*ut steak into bite-size pieces. Cook and stir steak, onion, and garlic in oil in a large saucepan over medium heat until brown. Drain off oil. Stir vinegar, water, chili sauce, paprika, chili powder, seasoned salt, soy sauce, and mushrooms into steak mixture. Bring to a boil; reduce heat. Cover and simmer for 1 hour or until meat is tender. Cool and store in freezer container.

To prepare for serving, thaw meat mixture and heat in saucepan until bubbly. Cook egg noodles according to package directions. Stir sour cream or low-fat yogurt and flour together; combine with stroganoff. Heat to a boil, stirring constantly. Reduce heat; simmer and stir about 1 minute. Serve stroganoff over noodles. Makes 6 to 8 servings.

Summary of processes: Cut steak in bite-size pieces; chop 1 cup onion; mince 2 cloves garlic

Freeze in: 6-cup container

Serve with: Tomatoes stuffed with guacamole, corn on the cob

RECIPES

BAKED BEANS AND HAMBURGER

3 strips bacon, diced
¾ pound lean ground beef (2 cups browned)
1¼ cups finely chopped onion (or ½ cup sautéed)
1 31-ounce can pork and beans in tomato sauce
1 8-ounce can tomato sauce
¼ cup brown sugar
1 tablespoon prepared mustard
¼ cup catsup
Salt and pepper to taste

*B*rown bacon; drain on a paper towel. In a large skillet, brown ground beef and sauté onion until tender. Mix in bacon and remaining ingredients, put in container, and freeze.

To prepare for serving, thaw beans and hamburger and preheat oven to 350°. Place mixture in a large baking dish that has been treated with nonstick spray; bake, uncovered, for 30 to 45 minutes. Makes 6 servings.

Summary of processes: Dice ¼ pound bacon; chop 1¼ cups onion

Freeze in: 5-cup container

Serve with: Swedish Rye Bread (page 184), corn on the cob, tossed green salad

BALKAN MEATBALLS

1 egg
¼ cup milk
⅓ cup crushed seasoned croutons
¾ teaspoon salt
¾ teaspoon sugar
¼ teaspoon ground ginger
¼ teaspoon ground nutmeg
¼ teaspoon ground allspice
1 pound lean ground beef
½ pound ground turkey
⅔ cup finely chopped onion
1 8-ounce package wide egg noodles*
2 tablespoons margarine*
¼ cup all-purpose flour*
2 cups milk*
Parsley for garnish*

*P*reheat oven to broil and/or 550°. In a medium mixing bowl, beat egg with milk. Mix in crushed croutons, salt, sugar, and spices. Add beef, turkey, and onion; mix thoroughly. Shape meat mixture into meatballs the size of walnuts. Place meatballs on a rimmed cookie sheet; broil until lightly browned. Cool; put meatballs in a large bag, and freeze them.

To prepare for serving, thaw meatballs. Cook noodles according to package directions. At the same time, make white sauce in a large skillet. Melt margarine over low heat. Add flour, stirring constantly until mixture is smooth and bubbly. Gradually stir in milk. Heat to a boil over medium heat, stirring constantly. Boil and stir 1 minute until thick and smooth. Add meatballs to sauce. Bring to a boil; reduce heat. Cover pan; simmer 15 minutes, stirring occasionally. Serve meatballs and sauce over wide egg noodles. Chop parsley; sprinkle over top. Makes 4 servings.

Summary of processes: Chop ⅔ cup onion

Freeze in: 1-gallon bag

Serve with: Cooked green beans, Mimi's Nutritious Bread (page 181)

SICILIAN MEAT ROLL

2 slightly beaten eggs
¾ cup soft bread crumbs (1 slice)
½ cup tomato juice
2 tablespoons snipped parsley
½ teaspoon dried oregano, crushed
¼ teaspoon salt
¼ teaspoon pepper
1 teaspoon minced garlic (1 clove)
2 pounds lean ground beef
6 1-ounce thin slices fully cooked ham
1¾ cups grated mozzarella cheese (7 ounces)

*I*n a large bowl combine eggs, bread crumbs, tomato juice, parsley, oregano, salt, pepper, and garlic. Stir in the ground beef, mixing well. On waxed paper, pat meat mixture into a 12x10-inch rectangle. Arrange ham slices atop meat, leaving a ¾-inch border around all edges. Sprinkle 1½ cups of the grated mozzarella cheese over ham. Starting from a short end, carefully roll up meat, using waxed paper to lift; seal edges and ends. Seal in a freezer bag; label and freeze.

Thaw roll and preheat oven to 350°. When thawed, place roll, seam-side down, in a 13x9x2-inch baking pan. Bake for 1 hour and 15 minutes or until temperature registers 170° and juices run clear. (Center of meat roll will be pink because of the ham.) Sprinkle remaining grated mozzarella over top of roll. Return to the oven for 5 minutes more or until cheese melts. Makes 8 to 10 servings.

Summary of processes: Tear one slice soft bread into crumbs; mince 1 clove garlic; slice thin 6 ounces ham; grate 1¾ cups mozzarella cheese

Freeze in: 1-gallon bag

Serve with: Cranberry sauce, rolls

CHAPTER SIX

GREEN CHILI ENCHILADAS

1½ pounds lean ground beef (3¾ cups browned meat)
1¼ cups finely chopped onion (¾ cup sautéed)
1 tablespoon chili powder
Salt and pepper to taste
8 to 12 flour tortillas
2 cups grated Monterey Jack cheese (1 cup*)
1 10¾-ounce can condensed cream of chicken soup
1½ cups sour cream
1 4-ounce can diced, green chilies

*B*rown ground beef and sauté onion. Combine with chili powder, salt, and pepper. Reserve 1 cup cheese in a 1-quart freezer bag to use when serving. Spoon enough meat mixture and cheese on each tortilla to cover a third of it. Roll tortilla beginning at the filled edge. Place seam-side down in a 13x9x2-inch baking dish treated with nonstick spray. When tortillas are completed, combine soup, sour cream, and green chilies to make a sauce; pour over tortillas. Cover dish with foil, and freeze with bag of cheese taped to it.

To prepare for serving, thaw enchiladas and cheese and preheat oven to 375°. Bake, uncovered, for 20 to 25 minutes. The last 10 minutes sprinkle cheese on top. Makes 8 servings.

Summary of processes: Chop 1¼ cups onion; grate 3 cups Monterey Jack cheese

Freeze in: 1-quart bag; 13x9x2-inch baking dish

Serve with: Spanish rice, Salsa De Lentejas (page 199)

JACK BURGERS

1 pound lean ground beef
½ teaspoon onion salt
¼ teaspoon freshly ground black pepper
4 thin slices Monterey Jack cheese
4 hamburger buns*

*F*orm ground beef into 8 thin patties. Sprinkle onion salt and black pepper over them. Place a slice of cheese on four of the patties. Cover each with another patty, pinching to seal cheese inside. Freeze in a 1-gallon freezer bag with waxed paper between each set of patties.

To serve, thaw patties and buns. Grill or fry to desired doneness. Makes 4 servings.

Summary of processes: Cut 4 slices Monterey Jack cheese

Freeze in: 1-gallon bag

Serve with: Pasta salad, root beer floats

CHAPTER SIX

BIRD'S NEST PIE

1 16-ounce package spaghetti (use half)
2 eggs, beaten
⅓ cup grated Parmesan cheese
½ cup finely chopped onion (¼ cup sautéed)
2 tablespoons margarine or butter
1 8-ounce carton sour cream (1 cup)
1 pound bulk Italian or turkey sausage (2½ cups browned)
1 6-ounce can tomato paste
1 cup water
4 ounces sliced mozzarella cheese

*B*reak spaghetti in half, and cook as directed on package until al dente; drain. While spaghetti is warm, combine with eggs and Parmesan cheese. Use a spoon to press spaghetti into bottom and up sides of a well-greased, 10-inch pie plate. Sauté onion in margarine, mix with sour cream, and spread over crust.

At the same time, brown sausage in a large skillet; drain fat. Stir in tomato paste and water. Bring to a boil; reduce heat. Simmer, uncovered, for 10 minutes, stirring occasionally. Spoon over sour cream mixture. Cover dish with foil and freeze. Put cheese slices in a 1-quart bag; attach to side of dish.

To prepare for serving, thaw pie and cheese and preheat oven to 350°. Bake pie, uncovered, for 25 minutes. Arrange mozzarella slices on top; return pie to oven until cheese melts. Makes 8 servings.

Summary of processes: Chop ½ cup onion; slice 4 ounces mozzarella cheese

Freeze in: 10-inch quiche or pie plate; 1-quart bag

Serve with: Strawberry gelatin, cooked fresh broccoli

Note: If you double this recipe, use 3 9-inch pie plates.

RECIPES

SAUSAGE AND RICE

1 6¼-ounce box fast-cooking long grain and wild rice
1 pound bulk Italian or turkey sausage
1¼ cups finely chopped onion (1 cup sautéed)
1 8-ounce can sliced water chestnuts, drained
1 cup chopped green bell pepper
1 cup chopped celery
1 4-ounce can mushroom stems and pieces
1 10¾-ounce can cream of mushroom soup
¾ teaspoon salt

*C*ook rice according to package directions. Brown sausage; drain fat. Sauté onion. Combine rice, onion, sausage, and remaining ingredients; put in a 1-gallon bag and freeze.

To prepare for serving, thaw sausage and rice mixture and preheat oven to 350°. Put mixture in a baking dish that has been treated with nonstick spray; bake, uncovered, for 1 hour. Makes 6 servings.

Summary of processes: Chop 1¼ cups onion, 1 cup green bell pepper, 1 cup celery

Freeze in: 1-gallon bag

Serve with: Cinnamon Applesauce Salad (page 197), carrot and celery sticks

Note: This is quite spicy, so it isn't suitable for someone who is sick.

CHICKEN TETRAZZINI

1 16-ounce package (use half) spaghetti
1¼ cups finely chopped onion (1 cup sautéed)
3 tablespoons margarine
1 cup chopped green bell pepper
5½ cups cooked, chopped chicken
4 cups grated Monterey Jack cheese
2 10¾-ounce cans cream of mushroom soup
1 10¾-ounce soup can milk
Salt and pepper to taste

*B*reak spaghetti in half and cook as directed on package until al dente; drain. Sauté onion in margarine. Thoroughly mix onion and remaining ingredients with spaghetti in a large bowl. Put spaghetti mixture in 2 containers and freeze.

To prepare for serving, thaw tetrazzini and preheat oven to 350°. Put mixture in a baking dish that has been treated with nonstick spray. Bake, uncovered, until bubbly, about 30 to 40 minutes. Makes 12 servings.

Summary of processes: Chop 5½ cups cooked chicken; chop 1 cup green bell pepper and 1¼ cup onion; grate 4 cups Monterey Jack cheese

Freeze in: 2 6-cup containers

Serve with: Fresh-Baked Asparagus (page 200), Spring Cake (page 195)

Note: Serve half the Chicken Tetrazzini; take the other half to a family with a new baby or a special need. Include applesauce and cake.

DEBORAH'S SWEET AND SOUR CHICKEN

½ cup sugar
3 tablespoons cornstarch
½ cup white vinegar
1 8-ounce can pineapple chunks (reserve juice)
¼ cup soy sauce
½ teaspoon salt
1 teaspoon minced garlic (1 clove)
½ teaspoon paprika
½ teaspoon ground ginger
1 cup coarsely chopped celery
1 cup coarsely chopped onion
3 cups cooked, chopped chicken
1 cup coarsely chopped green bell pepper
1 4-ounce can mushroom stems and pieces, drained
1 8-ounce can sliced water chestnuts, drained
2 cups regular, uncooked rice*

*I*n a medium saucepan, combine sugar and cornstarch; stir in white vinegar, juice from pineapple chunks, soy sauce, salt, garlic, paprika, ginger, celery, and onion. Bring to a boil; reduce heat. Simmer, stirring constantly until thickened. Remove from heat. Stir in pineapple chunks, chicken, bell pepper, mushrooms, and water chestnuts. Put in an 8-cup container and freeze.

To prepare for serving, thaw chicken and preheat oven to 350°. Put chicken in a baking dish treated with nonstick spray. Bake, uncovered, for 45 minutes. Prepare rice according to package directions. Serve chicken over rice. Makes 8 servings.

Summary of processes: Mince 1 clove garlic; coarsely chop 1 cup each onion, celery, and bell pepper; chop 3 cups cooked chicken

Freeze in: 8-cup container

Serve with: Tossed green salad, dinner rolls

Note: If you want to fill the house with a good aroma, this is the dish! You can also substitute leftover cooked pork for the chicken.

LEMON CHICKEN

1 teaspoon dried thyme leaves
1 teaspoon salt
½ teaspoon pepper
⅛ teaspoon garlic powder
⅓ cup lemon juice
1 pound raw chicken pieces
1 cup regular, uncooked rice*

*M*ix all the spices and lemon juice in a 1-gallon bag, add chicken pieces, and freeze. When thawed, preheat oven to 450°. Arrange chicken skin-side down in an 8x8x2-inch baking dish treated with nonstick spray. Pour liquid over chicken. Bake for 20 minutes. Turn chicken over and baste it. Bake 15 to 20 minutes more or until chicken is tender and no longer pink when cut along the bone. Prepare rice according to package directions. Serve chicken over rice. Makes 4 servings.

Freeze in: 1-gallon bag

Serve with: Cooked fresh broccoli, Blueberry Peach Fruit Crisp (page 193)

RECIPES

CHICKEN À LA KING

1 strip diced bacon
¼ cup finely chopped onion
1 2-ounce can mushroom stems and pieces (reserve ¼ cup liquid)
¼ cup chopped green bell pepper
1 tablespoon margarine or butter
¼ cup all-purpose flour
1 teaspoon salt
¼ teaspoon pepper
1 cup half-and-half
⅔ cup chicken broth
1 cup cooked, chopped chicken
1 tablespoon diced pimientos
1 package puff pastry shells*

*I*n a large saucepan, cook and stir bacon, onion, mushrooms, and bell pepper in margarine over medium heat until vegetables are tender. Blend in flour, salt, and pepper. Cook over low heat, stirring constantly until well mixed.

Remove from heat. Stir in half-and-half, chicken broth, and reserved mushroom liquid. Heat to a boil, stirring constantly for 1 minute. Stir in chicken and pimientos. Allow chicken mixture to cool, put in a 1-gallon bag, and freeze.

To prepare for serving, thaw puff pastry shells and chicken sauce. Heat sauce in large saucepan until bubbly, stirring constantly. Serve in warmed puff pastry shells. Makes 4 to 5 servings.

Summary of processes: Dice 1 strip bacon and 1 cup cooked chicken; chop ¼ cup onion and ¼ cup green bell pepper

Freeze in: 1-gallon bag

Serve with: Fresh-Baked Asparagus (page 200), red grapes or melon slices

CHICKEN BROCCOLI

1 10-ounce package frozen chopped broccoli
4 cups cooked, chopped chicken
1 10¾-ounce can condensed cream of chicken soup
½ cup light mayonnaise
1 4-ounce can mushroom stems and pieces, drained
¼ teaspoon curry powder
¾ cup grated Parmesan cheese

*C*ook broccoli in boiling water according to package directions. Drain broccoli, and spread in a 13x9x2-inch baking dish that has been treated with nonstick spray. Mix chicken, soup, mayonnaise, mushrooms, curry powder, and ½ cup Parmesan cheese in a medium bowl. Spread chicken mixture over broccoli. Sprinkle ¼ cup Parmesan cheese over top. Cover dish with foil and freeze.

To prepare for serving, thaw dish and preheat oven to 350°. Cover and bake for 40 minutes. Remove foil, stir to bring colder food in center to the outside; bake for 20 minutes more. Makes 6 servings.

Summary of processes: Chop 4 cups cooked chicken

Freeze in: 13x9x2-inch baking dish

Serve with: Croissants, Cranberry Cream Salad (page 196)

RECIPES

CHICKEN AND RICE PILAF

4 boneless, skinless chicken breasts
Salt, pepper, and paprika to taste
1¼ cups water or chicken broth
1 cup regular uncooked rice
½ package dry onion soup mix (¼ cup)
1 10¾-ounce can condensed cream of mushroom soup
2 tablespoons diced pimientos (½ of a 2-ounce jar)

*S*prinkle chicken breasts with salt, pepper, and paprika. Mix chicken broth, uncooked rice, onion soup mix, cream soup, and pimientos together; put in an 11x7x1½-inch baking dish that has been coated with nonstick spray. Place chicken breasts on top of rice mixture. Cover dish with foil and freeze.

To prepare for serving, thaw chicken dish and preheat oven to 375°. Bake, uncovered, for 1¼ hours or until chicken and rice are tender. Makes 4 servings.

Freeze in: 11x7x1½-inch baking dish

Serve with: Marinated Veggies (page 201), dinner rolls

ORIENTAL CHICKEN

2 tablespoons margarine
2 tablespoons all-purpose flour
1 cup chicken broth
1 cup water
1 tablespoon soy sauce
½ teaspoon garlic powder
2 cups cooked, chopped chicken
⅛ teaspoon pepper
1 5-ounce can chow mein noodles*

*M*elt margarine in a medium saucepan over low heat. Add flour and continue to stir over medium heat until bubbly. Add broth, water, soy sauce, garlic powder, chicken, and pepper; simmer for 5 minutes. Cool and freeze in a 1-gallon bag.

To prepare for serving, thaw chicken. Heat in a pan until bubbly. Serve over chow mein noodles. Makes 4 servings.

Summary of processes: Chop 2 cups cooked chicken

Freeze in: 1-gallon bag

Serve with: Egg rolls, fortune cookies

SPLIT PEA SOUP

12 ounces dry, green split peas
3 cups water
½ pound cooked, cubed ham
¾ teaspoon onion powder
⅛ teaspoon dried thyme leaves
⅛ teaspoon freshly ground pepper
⅓ cup chopped celery
¾ cup peeled and sliced carrots
1 cup finely chopped onion
1 bay leaf
Salt to taste

*R*inse split peas; soak them in cold water overnight; drain. Put peas with remaining ingredients in a large saucepan. Bring to a boil; reduce heat. Stirring occasionally, simmer about 2 hours until peas are tender and turn pasty. Cool and freeze in 6-cup container.

To serve, thaw peas, and simmer until warmed through. If peas are too thick, add water to make consistency of thick soup. Makes 6 servings.

Summary of processes: Soak split peas in water overnight; cut ham in cubes; peel and slice ¾ cup carrots; chop 1 cup onion and ¾ cup celery

Freeze in: 6-cup container

Serve with: Orange slices or canned peaches, cornbread

Salad Bowl Puff

Ham Salad Filling:
1 10-ounce package frozen peas (use half)
1 pound cooked, cubed ham (1 cup)
½ cup grated mild cheddar cheese
¾ teaspoon prepared mustard
1 tablespoon minced onion
⅓ cup light mayonnaise*

*R*inse peas under cold water to separate, but do not thaw; drain. Combine peas with ham, cheese, minced onion, and mustard. Put in a 1-gallon freezer bag and freeze.

To prepare for serving, thaw ham salad filling, and make the following pastry:

Pastry*:
⅓ cup plus 2 tablespoons water
½ cup biscuit baking mix
2 tablespoons margarine
2 eggs

*P*reheat oven to 400°. Spray an 8-inch pie plate with nonstick spray. Heat water and margarine to a boil in a 2-quart saucepan. Add baking mix all at once, stirring vigorously over low heat until mixture forms a ball, about 1½ minutes. Remove from heat. Beat in eggs one at a time, and continue beating until smooth. Spread mixture in bottom of pie pan (not sides). Bake pastry, uncovered, until puffed and dry in center, about 35 to 40 minutes. Cool pastry.

Just before serving, stir mayonnaise into cold ham mixture, fill pastry, and serve. Makes 4 servings.

Summary of processes: Cut 1 pound ham into cubes; grate ½ cup cheddar cheese

Freeze in: 1-gallon bag

Serve with: Lemon gelatin made with shredded carrots and crushed pineapple

MARINATED FLANK STEAK

½ cup vegetable oil
¼ cup soy sauce
¼ cup red wine vinegar
2 teaspoons Worcestershire sauce
½ teaspoon ground ginger
1 teaspoon minced garlic (1 clove)
1⅓ pounds flank steak

*M*ix first six ingredients for marinade. Put flank steak in a freezer bag, pour marinade over it, seal bag, and freeze.

To prepare for serving, thaw flank steak, remove from marinade, and barbecue 8 to 10 minutes per side; or set oven control to broil and/or 550°. Broil steak 6 inches from heat until brown, turning once, about 6 minutes on one side and 4 minutes on the other. Cut steak across grain at slanted angle into thin slices. Makes 4 servings.

Summary of processes: Mince 1 clove garlic

Freeze in: 1-gallon bag

Serve with: Twice-Baked Potatoes Deluxe (page 200), cooked zucchini

SHISH KEBABS

2 pounds cubed, boneless, top sirloin steak
¾ cup coarsely chopped onion
1 4-ounce can green chili salsa
1½ teaspoons chili powder
1 tablespoon vegetable oil
¼ cup red wine vinegar
¼ teaspoon salt
Pepper to taste
½ green bell pepper*
1 onion*
4 ounces whole fresh mushrooms*
Half-pint box cherry tomatoes*
½ of 1 8-ounce can pineapple chunks
1 cup regular, uncooked rice*

*C*ombine cubed beef with chopped onion, salsa, chili powder, oil, red wine vinegar, salt, and pepper; put in a 6-cup container and freeze.

To prepare for serving, thaw meat mixture. Remove meat from marinade. Cut bell pepper and onion into thick pieces to put on a skewer. Alternate meat, vegetables, and pineapple on a skewer, and barbecue or broil. Baste with marinade while cooking. At the same time, prepare rice according to package directions. Serve kebabs with rice. Makes 4 servings.

Summary of processes: Cut steak into cubes; chop ½ bell pepper and 1½ cups onion into thick pieces

Freeze in: 6-cup container

Serve with: Corn on the cob, Spring Cake (page 195)

Note: Serve these the first week; otherwise, fresh vegetables will spoil.

RECIPES

GRILLED FISH

1¼ pounds frozen fish fillets (halibut, swordfish, or orange roughy)*
5 to 6 new potatoes*
½ cup soy sauce
¼ cup water
¼ chicken bouillon cube
2 tablespoons olive oil
1 tablespoon brown sugar
2 teaspoons minced garlic (2 cloves)
½ teaspoon ground ginger

$\mathcal{F}$reeze fish fillets and store new potatoes until you're ready to serve them. Whisk remaining ingredients in a small bowl to make marinade. Freeze in a plastic bag taped to fish fillet package.

To prepare for serving, thaw marinade and fish fillets. Marinate fish for 30 minutes. Prepare new potatoes. Heat 1 cup salted water to a boil; add potatoes. Cover, heat until boiling; reduce heat. Simmer, tightly covered, until tender, 30 to 35 minutes; drain.

At the same time, remove fish from marinade. Set oven control to broil and/or 550°. Broil or grill fish for 10 minutes per inch of thickness or until fish flakes easily with a fork. Baste frequently with marinade while cooking. If fish is more than 1-inch thick, turn once during cooking. Makes 4 servings.

Summary of processes: Mince 2 garlic cloves

Freeze in: 1-quart bag taped to fish fillet package

Serve with: Tossed green salad

CHAPTER SIX

CRUSTLESS SPINACH QUICHE

1 10-ounce package frozen chopped spinach
1 bunch chopped green onion bulbs (without greens)
4 eggs
1 16-ounce carton low-fat cottage cheese
2 cups grated mild cheddar cheese
¼ cup crouton crumbs*

*C*ook spinach according to package directions, and squeeze to remove liquid. Combine spinach, green onions, eggs, cottage cheese, and cheddar cheese. Put into a quiche pan or 10-inch pie plate treated with nonstick spray. Cover with foil and freeze. Put crouton crumbs in a 1-quart bag and tape to pie plate.

To prepare for serving, thaw pie and crumbs and preheat oven to 325°. Bake, uncovered, for 1 hour, adding crouton crumbs the last 15 minutes. Makes 8 servings.

Summary of processes: Chop 1 bunch green onions; grate 2 cups cheddar cheese; crush croutons to make ¼ cup

Freeze in: 10-inch quiche pan or pie plate; 1-quart bag

Serve with: Fresh sliced tomatoes, Banana-Sauce Muffins (page 185)

Note: This dish is nice for a ladies' luncheon.

JAN'S SANDWICHES

1 2½-ounce package thin-sliced, corned beef luncheon meat
1 8-ounce jar Cheez Whiz
1 tablespoon minced onion
2 tablespoons light mayonnaise
8 sandwich or onion rolls

*C*hop corned beef and mix with Cheez Whiz, onion, and mayonnaise. Spread filling on one bun; top with second bun. Wrap buns individually in foil and freeze.

To prepare for serving, thaw rolls and preheat oven to 350°. Bake in foil for 20 minutes. Makes 8 servings.

Summary of processes: Chop corned beef

Freeze in: Foil wrap

Serve with: Chips, fresh fruit salad

SAUCY HOT DOGS

2 cups Grandma's Chili*
6 hot dog buns*
6 hot dogs or turkey franks*

*T*haw frozen chili, hot dogs, and buns. Cook hot dogs in a small amount of water until heated through; drain, and cut lengthwise. Heat chili in a saucepan until bubbly. If desired, heat buns. Put hot dogs in buns and smother with chili. Makes 6 servings.

Freeze in: 2-cup container

Serve with: Corn chips, cottage cheese, sliced pineapple, mandarin oranges

GRILLED HAM SLICES

2 pounds cooked ham* cut in 2 ¾-inch-thick center slices
1 cup regular, uncooked rice*
¾ cup brown sugar*
1 tablespoon prepared mustard*
2 teaspoons water*
1 tablespoon vinegar or lemon juice*

*F*reeze ham slices in 1-gallon bag. To serve, thaw ham slices. Prepare rice according to package directions. Mix remaining ingredients for glaze, and spread over ham slices. Grill, broil, or barbecue ham slices 2 or 3 minutes per side, basting with sauce once per side. Makes 4 servings.

Freeze in: 1-gallon bag

Serve with: Cinnamon Applesauce Salad (page 197), Twice-Baked Potatoes (page 200)

OVEN BARBECUED CHICKEN AND CHEESY BISCUITS

2½ pounds chicken pieces*
½ cup grated mild cheddar cheese*
1 cup barbecue sauce (your favorite brand)*
1 12-ounce package Hungry Jack buttermilk biscuits*

*F*reeze chicken in a 1-gallon bag and cheddar cheese in a 1-quart bag. Refrigerate sauce and biscuits until serving day.

To serve, thaw chicken and grated cheese. Preheat oven to 400°. Treat a 13x9x2-inch baking dish with nonstick spray. Dip chicken pieces in barbecue sauce. Place them in pan, skin-side up. Bake for 40 to 45 minutes. Pile chicken pieces at one end of pan. Separate dough into 10 biscuits. Place them in the pan in drippings next to chicken. Sprinkle cheese over biscuits. Bake for 15 to 20 minutes until biscuits are golden brown. Makes 5 servings.

Summary of processes: Grate ½ cup cheddar cheese

Freeze in: 1-gallon and 1-quart bags

Serve with: Baked beans, cole slaw

CHAPTER SEVEN
Table Talk Questions

*B*e wise in the way you act.
Let your conversation be
always full of grace,
seasoned with salt.

Colossians 4:5a, 6

*D*inner table conversation builds a sense of security and family identity in children and helps us get to know one another better as we tune into each other's day. In addition, studies of students who excel in school point to the benefit of directed conversation at a family dinner table, where each family member has his or her say and then waits to hear the views of others.

Try some of these topics with your family—and with company too.

TABLE TALK QUESTIONS AND CONVERSATION STARTERS

1. Tell about one thing you started today, and one thing you finished.
2. Is faster always better? Talk about some times it is and some times it isn't.
3. What worries you most?
4. Of what are you proudest?
5. If you could do anything you want for a career, what would it be?
6. Give a sincere compliment to the person on your right.
7. What responsibilities do you think parents have to their children?
8. Which of your friends' parents do you respect most and why?
9. What does it mean to be patriotic?
10. What would you most like to change about yourself?
11. Read off a list of state capitals. Going around the table, each person must try to match the state with the capital.
12. Start a story. After a few sentences, pass to the next person to add to the story and so on around the table.
13. (With young children) Tell us about the picture you drew today.
14. (With young children) Sing a song.
15. Discuss upcoming events of lifestyle changes that will affect your family, for example, a new job, a new grade, failing health of grandparents.
16. What is one new thing you'd like to try?
17. Where is one place you'd like to go?
18. How can you help people in your work?
19. What is your favorite fragrance?

20. If you ran for a political office, what would it be? What would be your central campaign issue?

21. Tell about a time you broke a bone or were injured in some way.

22. What is a favorite song of yours?

23. Let a child who plays an instrument give a brief concert: one child per night.

24. Mom and Dad tell what they worried about most and what they liked most when they were children.

25. Ask grandparents to reminisce about colorful characters in their families.

26. What are some of your family traditions?

27. Play family trivia: Where did Dad and Mom meet? How many second cousins do you have? What was the name of your first pet?

28. Talk about salaries. Give five or six examples of average earnings for various occupations. Do wages necessarily match the value or significance of the work done?

29. Share a memory that goes way, way back in your childhood.

30. What is the best thing that happened to you today? The worst thing?

31. What is the funniest thing that happened to you today?

32. Where did you see God at work today?

33. Bring a newspaper clipping and discuss a character quality it exemplified, i.e., greed, courage, disregard for human life.

34. Tell a favorite memory from a wedding you attended.

35. Read excerpts from a letter recently written to the family.

36. What was the most interesting thing you learned today?

37. Tell about the main character in a book you're reading and the challenge he or she is facing.

38. What is the saddest movie or television show that you have watched?

39. Who Does It Belong to Night: Bring out of a bag out-of-place objects one by one. Who does it belong to? (Keep it light.) Does it work? Do you want to keep it? Then you may be excused to quickly put it way. (Try to anticipate and avoid arguments over ownership.)

40. Why are some people liked and some are not?

41. What is the difference between natural talents and spiritual gifts?

42. What would be your ideal vacation?

43. What is your favorite Christmas decoration? How did it become special to you?

44. Find and read a poem expressive of the current season.
45. Tell what someone said today that made you feel good about yourself.
46. If you were the opposite sex, what would be the hardest adjustment?
47. If you could change one physical feature, what would it be?
48. What is/was your nickname?
49. What characteristics do you see in you that came from your father/mother?
50. What qualities would you like to emulate from your parents/relatives?
51. Who is your favorite relative?
52. If you won the lottery, how would it change your life?
53. Tell about a time you were frightened.
54. Discuss the doctrine of election vs. free will.
55. Discuss what elements are included in a home mortgage. How does life insurance work?
56. Discuss what one should do if involved in a car accident.
57. Discuss how to shut off the water to the house.
58. Devise a family plan for evacuation of your home in case of fire.
59. Role-play appropriate phone-answering and message-taking procedures.
60. Take a saying like "Start at the top and work down." Think of as many applications for it as you can.
61. Which holiday has the most meaning for you and why?
62. How do different types of music affect you?
63. What was your favorite childhood storybook? Why did you like it?
64. What is your favorite time of the day? Your favorite season?
65. Where do you want to be in ten years?
66. What disability do you fear the most?
67. Tell about a figure in literature (or on television) who has impacted your life.
68. Plan a vacation with one boat, two weeks, four other people, and $10,000.
69. If you could live in a different century, what century would it be?
70. For what purpose were you born?
71. If you were invisible, who would you like to observe?
72. If you were invisible, what conversation would you like to hear?
73. If you were the opposite sex, what would you want to do first?
74. If you could change your name, what name would you choose and why?

75. If you could be a professional in sports, what sport would you choose?

76. Plan a favorite dinner party. What food would you serve? Who would you invite? Where would you have the party?

77. If you could own a store, what kind would it be?

78. If you had four eyes, where would you put the other two?

79. If you had one minute to grab something of value as your house burned, what would it be?

80. (With children) Have one family member cover both eyes. Let the rest of the family help that person eat. Talk about how it would be to be blind.

81. (With children) Put a cotton ball in each ear. Then cover the ears with a wool hat. Discuss what it would be like to be hearing impaired.

82. If you could be a bird, which one would you choose and why? An animal?

83. (With children) What does a fireman (or other occupation) have in his/her pocket?

84. (With children) What is the hardest part of a teacher's job?

85. (With children) If you could be like any older person, who would you be like?

86. (With children) What would you do with your time if you didn't have a television?

87. (With children) What would you like to ask the President (or another historical figure)?

88. What would you like to ask your great-grandparents?

89. Each person chooses a letter of the alphabet. How many animals can you name beginning with your letter?

90. What do you think would make God laugh?

91. (With children) What did Jesus like most when he was your age?

92. (With children) If you could take Jesus to your school for one hour, what would you show him?

93. What do you like best/worst about being your age?

94. (With children) If you could fly, where would you go?

95. What is one of the best gifts you have ever given?

96. What is a favorite memory you have with your parent or sibling?

97. If you could give $1,000 away, to whom would you give it?

98. What is the nicest thing you've done recently for an elderly or disabled person?

99. What would you miss most if you lost the sense of smell?

100. (With children) If your pet could talk, what would it say?

101. If you could have a Bible (or movie) character come to your house, who would it be?

102. (With children) What Bible or movie character is most like your parent/sibling?

103. Set an extra place at the table. Then ask the question "What would you ask Jesus if he came for dinner?"

104. What would you miss most if you were stranded in the mountains for two weeks?

105. (With children) "Sticks and stones can break my bones. . . ." What words have hurt you?

106. If you were caught in a snowstorm, in the car, with a winter coat, what would you do to survive?

107. (With children) Most uniforms include a hat. Which uniform hat do you like the most?

108. Why are churches usually built to be beautiful?

109. (With children) Suppose you were "home alone." In your piggy bank you have $1.29. What would you do?

110. What part of your body are you thrilled with?

111. If you could buy any car, what would it be?

112. While walking on a beach, you find a newborn baby boy. He's having trouble breathing. What would you do?

113. Other than water, what do you think is the most common drink in the world?

114. "Over the river and through the woods to Grandmother's house we go." What landmarks do you remember that you pass on the way to your grandmother's house?

115. What are some objects that you particularly remember from a grandparent's house?

116. When you see the American flag, what do you think of?

117. Tell about your favorite birthday.

118. What is your favorite radio station and why?

119. Where is the most beautiful place you've ever been?

120. What was your favorite comic book super hero?

121. Tell about a favorite memory of a grandparent.

122. If you have ever ridden on a train, tell about your ride.

123. What is your favorite flower? Your favorite tree?

124. Tell about a prize or an award you won.

125. If you were to live in another country for a year, what would you miss the most?

126. What foods do you most dislike?

127. Tell about a time when you were homesick.

128. Tell about a favorite teacher.

THANKSGIVING TABLE TALK

Give each guest a question that includes a letter from the word *Thanksgiving*.

129. Name Times this year when you saw the Lord working and this made you thankful.
130. What High points made you grateful?
131. What Announcements made you grateful?
132. What News made you thankful God was in charge?
133. What Kind act from someone made you thankful?
134. What Season most reminds you of God's goodness?
135. What Growth in your personal life with Christ made you thankful?
136. What Inherited quality about your personality made you grateful?
137. What Valuable lesson did you learn this year and why were you thankful?
138. What Inspirational thought did you have recently, and why did it make you grateful?
139. Name one blessing from this year that makes you thankful.
140. How would you describe Gratefulness?

TABLE TALK WITH INTERNATIONAL FRIENDS

141. What do you miss most about your country?
142. What things are difficult to adjust to here?
143. What have you enjoyed most in the U.S.?
144. Discuss how the guest's money corresponds with U.S. currency according to the exchange rate.
145. What games do children play in your country? Youth? Adult recreation?
146. What differences have you observed between schools here and there?
147. In what ways will you apply the education you are receiving when you return home?
148. Teach us to say some words in your language.
149. What is your favorite food in your country? In our country?
150. How do people in your culture worship? What are some of their religious customs?
151. What did you know about Christianity before you came here? Has anything you've learned about the Christian faith while you've been here surprised you? What?
152. How large is your family? What sort of work do your parents do?

CHAPTER EIGHT
More Recipes to Enhance Meals

*T*hey broke bread in their
homes and ate together with
glad and sincere hearts, praising
God and enjoying the favor of all
the people.

Acts 2:46b–47a

Even when you don't have to prepare an evening's entrée from scratch, it's easy to get into a rut over what to serve with it. Here are recipes to help round out your meals. They are easier to prepare because of the time you've saved with once-a-month cooking!

CHEESY-HERB BREAD

½ cup (1 stick) margarine
1 ¾-ounce package Good Seasons Cheese Garlic Salad Dressing
    Mix (or Garlic and Herb)
1½ cups grated mozzarella cheese
1 loaf French bread

*E*arly in the day, set out the ingredients so the margarine and mozzarella cheese can soften to room temperature.

After you have placed the day's entrée in the oven, combine margarine, salad dressing mix, and cheese until well blended; slice loaf of French bread and spread with mixture. Place on cookie sheet and put in oven for last 5 to 10 minutes of baking time of entrée. Or broil loaf for 3 to 5 minutes.

To prepare for baking at a later date, slice the French bread lengthwise into two halves and spread with mixture. Put the two halves back together and wrap securely with foil. Freeze.

When ready to serve, bake at 400° for 35 minutes. No need to thaw first. You can prepare several of these and have them available in your freezer for last-minute additions to any meal.

MIMI'S NUTRITIOUS BREAD

1 ¼-ounce package active dry yeast
3 cups lukewarm water
1 cup powdered milk
½ cup honey
4 cups whole wheat flour (may substitute 1 cup wheat germ for 1
    cup whole wheat flour)
1½ tablespoons salt
½ cup vegetable oil
5 to 6 cups all-purpose flour
Melted butter or margarine

*I*n a large mixing bowl dissolve yeast in lukewarm water. Add milk and honey and then 4 cups whole wheat flour. Beat with a whisk until lumps disappear (it will be about as thick as cake batter). Cover bowl with a towel, and let dough rise 60 minutes or until doubled in size.

Add salt and vegetable oil; beat in white flour, working all of it in until no longer sticky. Knead with a dough hook 3 to 4 minutes or 10 minutes by hand, until dough is smooth. Put dough in a large, greased bowl, turning it once to grease the top and bottom. Cover bowl with a towel and let dough rise 50 minutes or until doubled in size.

Punch dough down and let it rise 40 more minutes or until doubled in size. Divide dough in half and shape into 2 large, smooth loaves. Grease pans with vegetable shortening and put loaves in pans. Cover pans with a towel and let dough rise 30 minutes or until doubled in size. Set timer for 15 minutes to remind yourself to preheat oven to 350°. Bake for 1 hour. Remove loaves from oven; brush tops with melted butter or margarine. Makes 2 loaves.

Dinner Rolls: Divide dough in half, making one half into a loaf. Make dinner rolls out of the other half by rolling dough into a long tube about 2 inches thick. Cut the tube at 2-inch sections; roll each piece into a round ball. Bake rolls on a cookie sheet in a preheated 350° oven for 25 to 30 minutes. Rub a cube of butter over the tops of warm rolls.

Cheddar-Beef Rolls: Form dough into balls according to the above directions; then flatten balls into circles about the size of your palm. Fold each circle of dough around a small wedge of cheddar cheese and 2 tablespoons browned ground beef. Preheat oven to 350°. Bake sealed-side down on a cookie sheet for 25 to 30 minutes.

To serve, put barbecue sauce in individual serving dishes. Dip rolls in sauce. These are great for lunch.

MORE RECIPES — BREADS

PORTUGUESE SWEET BREAD

2 packages active dry yeast
1⅔ cups warm water
1 cup dry instant potato flakes
1 cup sugar
6 tablespoons (⅔ stick) melted margarine or butter
2 teaspoons salt
4 eggs
1 tablespoon finely shredded lemon or orange zest, or ½ tablespoon
    each
¾ cup raisins
¾ cup golden raisins
7½ cups all-purpose flour

*I*n a large mixing bowl soften yeast in warm water. Mix in potato flakes, sugar, melted margarine, salt, eggs, citrus zest, and raisins. Add flour until dough is no longer sticky, about 7½ cups. Knead with dough hook 2 to 3 minutes or by hand 10 minutes, until smooth. Put dough in a large, greased bowl, turning it once to grease on top and bottom. Cover bowl with a towel.

Let dough rise 1½ hours or until doubled in size. Punch it down and let it rise 10 minutes more. Divide dough into 3 large, round loaves or 4 smaller ones; place them on a greased cookie sheet with space between them. You can also braid the dough or form it into any shape.

Cover dough with a towel, and allow it to rise until almost doubled in size, about 45 minutes. Preheat oven at 350°. Bake loaves for 35 to 40 minutes, depending on number of loaves. Cover them with foil after the first 20 minutes so they won't get too brown. Makes 3 or 4 loaves.

Note: This bread makes great toast. We enjoy giving these festive loaves to our neighbors for Christmas.

DAWN'S FRENCH BREAD

3 cups warm water
1 ¼-ounce package active dry yeast
3 tablespoons sugar
1½ tablespoons salt
7½ to 8 cups all-purpose flour, divided

*I*n a large mixing bowl dissolve yeast in 1 cup warm water. Add sugar and salt; let stand 5 minutes. Stir in 2 cups water and 3 cups flour, beating with the paddle on a heavy-duty mixer or by hand with a wooden spoon.

Add remaining flour a cup at a time. Knead with dough hook 4 to 6 minutes or 8 to 10 minutes by hand, until the dough feels smooth and elastic. Cover with a towel; let dough rise until almost tripled in size. Or make dough early in the morning, and let it rise all day. Shape dough into 4 baguettes (long, slender loaves). Let loaves rise about 45 minutes until doubled in size. Preheat oven to 450°. Bake for 15 minutes. Reduce temperature to 350°; bake for 30 minutes more or until golden brown. Makes 4 loaves.

Note: Freeze each baked loaf in foil. To reheat, loosen one end of foil and heat loaf at 375° until hot and crisp—about 20 minutes. You may also want to use this dough for Pizza Roll-Ups or Veggie Pizza instead of commercial frozen dough.

SWEDISH RYE BREAD

2 ¼-ounce packages active dry yeast
¼ cup plus 1 teaspoon sugar, divided
9½ cups all-purpose flour, divided
2 cups warm water, divided
2 cups milk
5 tablespoons soft margarine
½ cup brown sugar
½ cup molasses
1 tablespoon salt
1¼ teaspoons anise seed
2 teaspoons caraway seed
3 cups rye flour
3 tablespoons dark corn syrup

*C*ombine yeast, 1 teaspoon sugar, 1½ cups all-purpose flour, and 1 cup warm water in a small bowl. Cover and let rise about 30 minutes.

In a small saucepan, scald 2 cups milk combined with remaining cup of warm water. Combine margarine, brown sugar, ¼ cup white sugar, molasses, salt, anise seed, caraway seed, 1 cup all-purpose flour, rye flour, and dark corn syrup in a large bowl. Stir scalded milk into this mixture. Let it cool until warm to the touch. Stir in yeast mixture. Gradually stir in about 3 cups all-purpose flour until a ball forms. Then turn dough onto a hard surface and gradually mix in 4 more cups flour, kneading dough 8 to 10 minutes until it's smooth and elastic. Put dough into a greased bowl and cover with a towel; let rise until doubled in size, about 50 minutes.

Divide dough to make 3 or 4 loaves. Put them in greased loaf pans, or shape dough into 5 or 6 small loaves and bake them on ungreased cookie sheets.

Let loaves rise about 45 minutes. Preheat oven to 325°. Bake for about 40 to 50 minutes, depending on size and number of loaves. Rub a butter cube over tops of the warm loaves. Remove them from pans immediately and cool. Makes 3 to 4 regular loaves or 5 to 6 small loaves.

Note: These loaves are excellent as an alternative to cookies and fudge for Christmas gifts.

BANANA-SAUCE MUFFINS

1¼ cups all-purpose flour
1½ cups quick-cooking oatmeal
⅓ cup sugar
1 teaspoon baking powder
¾ teaspoon baking soda
½ teaspoon salt
1 banana, mashed
applesauce
1 egg
⅓ cup dark brown sugar
⅓ cup milk
¼ cup vegetable oil
1 teaspoon vanilla extract

Preheat oven to 350°. In mixing bowl, combine flour, oatmeal, sugar, baking powder, soda, and salt. Place mashed banana in 1-cup measure; add enough applesauce to make 1 cup. Combine banana-applesauce mixture with egg, brown sugar, milk, oil, and vanilla. Add liquid ingredients to dry ingredients all at once; stir just until moistened. Spoon into paper-lined muffin pans. Bake for 15 to 18 minutes. Makes 1 dozen.

These muffins freeze well. Cool muffins thoroughly and wrap each muffin in plastic wrap before placing them into a freezer bag.

APPLE-DATE FREEZER COFFEE CAKE

Topping:
⅔ cup firmly packed dark brown sugar
½ cup chopped walnuts or pecans
1 teaspoon cinnamon
2 tablespoons butter or margarine, melted

Cake ingredients:
½ cup (1 stick) butter or margarine, softened
¾ cup sugar
2 eggs
1 cup sour cream
1 teaspoon vanilla extract
2 cups all-purpose flour
1 teaspoon baking powder
1 teaspoon baking soda
½ teaspoon salt
1 large Golden Delicious apple, cored and coarsely grated (use mini processor)
½ cup chopped dates

*G*rease a 9x9-inch baking pan. Combine topping ingredients in small bowl; set aside. In a large bowl with mixer at medium speed, beat butter with sugar until light and fluffy. Add eggs, sour cream, and vanilla; beat until well blended. In separate bowl, combine flour, baking powder, soda, and salt. Stir dry ingredients into creamed mixture; blend. Stir in apple and dates. Pour into prepared pan. Sprinkle evenly with topping. Wrap tightly with foil and freeze.

About 1½ hours before serving, preheat oven to 350°. Bake frozen coffee cake, uncovered, for 60 to 65 minutes or until toothpick inserted in center comes out clean. Serve warm, or cool in pan for serving later. Makes 9 servings.

CHAPTER EIGHT

CINNAMON LOGS

2 egg yolks
1¾ cups sugar, divided
2 8-ounce packages cream cheese, softened
3 loaves Pepperidge Farm sandwich bread (or other very firm, thin-
    sliced white bread)
1 pound (4 sticks) margarine
4 teaspoons ground cinnamon

*P*reheat oven to 400°. Beat egg yolks and ½ cup sugar together; stir in cream cheese until smooth. Trim crusts from bread; use a rolling pin to flatten each slice.

Spread cheese mixture on a slice of bread; top with another slice to make a sandwich. Do the same with the remaining bread slices. Cut each sandwich lengthwise into 4 logs.

Melt margarine. Mix cinnamon and remaining 1¼ cups sugar in a bowl. Dip each log in melted margarine, and then in cinnamon sugar. Place on rimmed cookie sheets. Bake for 10 minutes. Makes 80 to 100 logs.

Note: Logs may also be frozen on rimmed cookie sheets; then put them in freezer bags. To serve, remove as many logs as you need from the bag. Put frozen logs on a cookie sheet or flat baking dish. Bake the same as above.

MORE RECIPES — BREADS

SPICY PUMPKIN MUFFINS

Muffin Batter:
1½ cups all-purpose flour
½ cup sugar
2 teaspoons baking powder
¾ teaspoon salt
1 teaspoon ground cinnamon
½ teaspoon ground ginger
¼ teaspoon ground cloves
½ cup raisins
1 egg
½ cup milk
½ cup canned pumpkin
¼ cup vegetable oil

Topping:
2½ teaspoons sugar
½ teaspoon ground cinnamon

*P*reheat to 400°. Stir flour, sugar, baking powder, salt, and spices in a large mixing bowl until well combined. Mix in raisins. Beat egg, milk, pumpkin, and oil in a smaller bowl. Pour pumpkin mixture into flour and spices, stirring only until combined. Fill lightly greased muffin cups ⅔ full. Mix sugar and cinnamon; sprinkle on muffins. Bake for 20 to 25 minutes or until nicely browned. Serve warm. Makes 12 muffins.

CHAPTER EIGHT

AUNTIE TEETO'S WAFFLES

**2 cups all-purpose flour (or substitute ½ cup whole wheat or buck-
    wheat flour for ½ cup of the all-purpose flour)**
1 teaspoon baking soda
1 teaspoon salt
2 eggs
1½ cups buttermilk
2 tablespoons vegetable oil
Maple syrup

*P*reheat waffle iron and spray with nonstick spray. Sift together flour, soda, and salt. In a medium bowl lightly beat eggs; stir in buttermilk and vegetable oil. Add liquid ingredients to flour mixture, stirring just to moisten. Pour a circle of batter about 5 inches in diameter into the center of a waffle iron. Bake according to waffle iron's instructions or until steaming stops, about 5 minutes. Serve with warmed maple syrup. Makes 6 servings.

Note: This recipe was given to Mimi by her ninety-four-year-old aunt, who used an equally old waffle iron. These waffles are great for Sunday supper for college students. Serve waffles with sausage and hot chocolate.

GOOD DAY GRANOLA

8 cups rolled oats (not instant)
1¼ cups firmly packed brown sugar
1½ cups unprocessed bran
1½ cups natural wheat germ (not toasted or honeyed)
¾ cup chopped walnuts
½ cup raw sunflower seeds
½ cup vegetable oil
¾ cup honey
2 teaspoons vanilla extract
2 cups raisins

Stir oats, brown sugar, bran, wheat germ, walnuts, and sunflower seeds in a large bowl. Put vegetable oil, honey, and vanilla in a small saucepan; heat, stirring until bubbly. Pour liquid over dry ingredients, mixing thoroughly. Preheat oven to 325°.

Divide oat mixture evenly and spread on two rimmed cookie sheets. Bake for 15 to 20 minutes, stirring once to keep granola evenly browned. While it cools, stir mixture several times to keep it from sticking together. When completely cool, add raisins. Store in an airtight container. Makes about 16 cups. — 32 - ½ c. sugr

Note: This granola keeps for weeks and is yummy for breakfast or snacks.

ORANGE SPICED TEA

2 cups powdered orange drink mix
¾ cup instant tea mix
1 teaspoon ground cinnamon
1 teaspoon ground cloves
1 2-quart package presweetened dry lemonade mix

*M*ix all the above ingredients together. To serve, stir 2 heaping teaspoons of the mix into an 8-ounce mug of hot water or a 10-ounce glass of cold water. This drink is great hot or cold.

CRANBERRY TEA

1 cup cranberry juice
3 cups prepared iced tea
3 tablespoons lemon juice
¼ cup sugar

*C*ombine all ingredients. Serve hot or cold. Makes 1 quart.

MORE RECIPES — BEVERAGES

BLUEBERRY PIE

1 10-ounce jar currant jelly
1 pint fresh blueberries
1 graham cracker crust, baked (see recipe below)
1 cup sour cream (or whipped topping for a sweeter pie)

*M*elt jelly in a saucepan over low heat. Add blueberries and stir. Pour into baked graham cracker crust. Spread sour cream on top and refrigerate overnight. Makes 6 to 8 servings.

Note: This pie is so easy and so good!

GRAHAM CRACKER CRUST

1½ cups crushed graham crackers
3 tablespoons sugar
⅓ cup (5 tablespoons plus 1 teaspoon) melted margarine or butter

*P*reheat oven to 350°. Crush graham crackers in a plastic bag, using a rolling pin. Mix crumbs with sugar and melted margarine. Press crumb mixture against bottom and sides of a 9-inch pie pan. Bake for 10 minutes.

BLUEBERRY PEACH FRUIT CRISP

Fruit Mixture:
1 16-ounce bag frozen peach slices (defrosted)
1 10-ounce box frozen blueberries (defrosted)
1 cup frozen apple juice concentrate (defrosted)
¼ cup minute tapioca
¾ teaspoon cinnamon

Topping:
1¾ cups fat-free granola (or low-fat granola), without fruit added
2 tablespoons frozen apple juice concentrate (defrosted)

*P*reheat oven to 350°. In an 8-inch square ovenproof glass baking dish, stir together peaches, blueberries, juice concentrate, tapioca, and cinnamon.

For topping, grind granola with juice concentrate in food processor or blender for about 2 minutes. Top fruit mixture with granola topping. Cover and bake for 30 minutes; remove cover and continue to bake additional 10 minutes until topping is lightly browned and fruit is tender. Cool on wire rack for 15 minutes. Serve warm or cold. Great served warm with frozen vanilla yogurt.

Note: This is a great winter dessert. You make it on the day you want to serve it, but you can freeze/store all the ingredients well in advance.

MORE RECIPES — DESSERTS

LOW-CALORIE CHOCOLATE CAKE

3 cups all-purpose flour
½ cup sugar
⅓ cup unsweetened cocoa powder
2 teaspoons baking soda
1 teaspoon salt
2 cups water
2 tablespoons white vinegar
4 teaspoons chocolate syrup
2 teaspoons vanilla extract
⅓ cup sugar
¾ cup (1½ sticks) margarine
2 teaspoons vegetable oil

*P*reheat oven to 350°. Mix flour, sugar, cocoa, baking soda, and salt; set aside. Mix water, vinegar, syrup, and vanilla in a separate bowl; set aside. Cream sugar, margarine, and vegetable oil in a large mixing bowl until fluffy. Alternate adding the dry and wet mixtures to the sugar and vegetable oil, beating well. Spray a Bundt pan with nonstick spray. Pour batter into Bundt pan and bake for 40 minutes. Serve with whipped cream or whipped topping, if desired.

SPRING CAKE

½ cup (1 stick) margarine
½ cup vegetable oil
¼ cup unsweetened cocoa powder
1 cup water
1 teaspoon baking soda
½ cup buttermilk
1 teaspoon ground cinnamon
2 cups all-purpose flour
2 cups sugar
2 eggs
1 teaspoon vanilla extract
½ teaspoon salt

*P*reheat oven to 400°. Bring margarine, vegetable oil, cocoa powder, and water to a boil in a large saucepan, stirring constantly. Remove pan from stove. Stir baking soda into buttermilk, adding to cocoa mixture along with cinnamon, flour, sugar, eggs, vanilla, and salt. Stir until well mixed. Pour batter into a greased and floured 13x9x2-inch baking pan. Bake for 20 to 25 minutes. Ice with Cocoa Frosting while cake is still warm. Makes 12 servings.

COCOA FROSTING

½ cup (1 stick) margarine
⅓ cup buttermilk
¼ cup unsweetened cocoa powder
1 16-ounce box confectioners' sugar
1 teaspoon vanilla extract
Nuts (optional)

*B*ring margarine, buttermilk, and cocoa to boil in a medium saucepan. Remove pan from heat. Beat in sugar and vanilla; while still warm pour on cake. Top with nuts, if desired.

Note: Bake this cake on the day a family member sees the first sign of spring. This cake and frosting freeze well.

JIFFY SALAD

Salad:
1 small head lettuce
2 to 3 hard-boiled eggs

Dressing:
¼ teaspoon salt
¼ teaspoon pepper
¼ cup vegetable oil
2 tablespoons vinegar
1 teaspoon soy sauce
1 tablespoon chopped fresh parsley
¼ cup grated Parmesan cheese

*W*ash and shred lettuce; put in a salad bowl. Chop eggs; add to lettuce. Mix remaining ingredients for dressing. Toss lettuce, eggs, and dressing. Makes 4 servings.

CRANBERRY CREAM SALAD

1 cup heavy whipping cream, chilled
3 tablespoons sugar
2 3-ounce packages cream cheese, softened
1 16-ounce can whole cranberry sauce
1 8-ounce can crushed pineapple, drained

*W*hip cream and sugar in a chilled bowl until stiff peaks form. Mix in remaining ingredients. Pour into a loaf pan and freeze. To serve, thaw slightly and cut into slices. Serve as a dessert or salad on lettuce leaves. Makes 8 to 10 servings.

CINNAMON APPLESAUCE SALAD

2 3-ounce packages lemon gelatin
½ cup red hots (cinnamon or candy imperials)
2 cups unsweetened applesauce
1 tablespoon lemon juice
Dash of salt

*D*issolve gelatin and red hots in 3 cups boiling water, stirring until they dissolve. Stir in applesauce, lemon juice, and salt. Chill until set in a square 8x8x1½-inch pan or gelatin mold. Makes 9 servings.

FROZEN FRUIT MEDLEY

1 17-ounce can apricots
1 20-ounce can unsweetened crushed pineapple
1 cup juice or syrup drained from apricots and pineapple
½ cup sugar
1 16-ounce package unsweetened, whole frozen strawberries
3 bananas, sliced
1 6-ounce can frozen orange juice concentrate
2 tablespoons lemon juice

*D*rain apricots and pineapple, reserving 1 cup of combined syrup. Cook syrup and sugar over medium heat about 5 minutes, stirring until sugar dissolves. Partially thaw strawberries until they can be separated. Add about 2 cups apricots, pineapple, strawberries, sliced bananas, syrup, orange juice concentrate, and lemon juice to the blender at a time. Cover and puree until smooth and slightly chunky; then pour each batch of fruit mixture into a large bowl. When all fruit has been blended, stir together. Line 30 muffin cups with paper baking cups. Ladle fruit mixture into paper cups. Freeze until solid.

When frozen, turn over muffin tins, and punch out frozen fruit cups with your thumb. Package frozen fruit cups in freezer bags. Remove cups from freezer 20 minutes before serving as a salad or dessert. Makes 30 servings.

Note: Put ice cream sticks in each cup before freezing to make sherbet treats.

MORE RECIPES — SALADS, SAUCES, SOUPS

HOT SPICED FRUIT

1 16-ounce can sliced peaches with syrup
1 16-ounce can pear halves with syrup
1 15-ounce can pineapple chunks with syrup
½ cup orange marmalade
1 3-inch cinnamon stick
½ teaspoon ground nutmeg
¼ teaspoon ground cloves

*M*ix all the above ingredients with liquid in a large saucepan. Bring to a boil; reduce heat. Cover and simmer 1 hour. Try fixing this in a Crockpot. Imagine the aroma! Makes 12 servings.

Note: Eat this warm as a fruit sauce, or it's good served over sliced ham or ice cream.

SMOKY CORN CHOWDER

½ cup chopped yellow onion
4 tablespoons (½ stick) butter or margarine
¼ cup all-purpose flour
1¼ teaspoons salt
¼ teaspoon pepper
4 cups milk
1 17-ounce can whole-kernel corn, drained
4 smoked sausage links, sliced (6-ounce package)
1 8-ounce can lima beans (optional)

*I*n a saucepan, sauté onion in butter until tender but not brown. Stir in flour, salt, and pepper. Add milk all at once. Bring to a boil, stirring constantly until thick and bubbly, about 1 minute. Stir in corn, sausage, and lima beans. Reduce heat; simmer 10 minutes. Makes 6 servings.

Note: Spread a picnic blanket on the floor, and have a family picnic in front of the fireplace on a winter night. Serve Smoky Corn Chowder with fresh-baked bread. Toast marshmallows for dessert.

SALSA DE LENTEJAS

⅔ cup chopped onion
1 scant teaspoon minced garlic (1 small clove)
1 tablespoon vegetable oil
¾ cup dried lentils, rinsed
2 cups water
2 beef bouillon cubes
⅛ teaspoon ground cayenne pepper
⅛ teaspoon freshly ground black pepper
½ teaspoon dried basil leaves, crumbled
½ teaspoon dried oregano leaves, crumbled
2 teaspoons white vinegar
1 8-ounce can tomato sauce
1 6-ounce can tomato paste

*I*n a large saucepan, sauté onion and garlic in vegetable oil for about 5 minutes. Add lentils, water, bouillon cubes, cayenne, and black pepper. Cover and simmer for 30 minutes. Add basil, oregano, vinegar, tomato sauce, and tomato paste, and simmer, uncovered, for about 1 hour, stirring occasionally. Makes 5 servings.

Note: This is a tasty but hot dish!

TWICE-BAKED POTATOES DELUXE

6 baking potatoes
Salt and pepper to taste
Margarine or butter
Milk
¼ cup chopped onion
¾ cup grated cheddar cheese
¾ cup grated Monterey Jack cheese
1 16-ounce box frozen, chopped spinach, thawed and pressed dry

*P*reheat oven to 400°. Prepare 6 baking potatoes and bake for 1 hour. Maintain oven temperature. While potatoes are still hot, slice each potato in half lengthwise. Carefully scoop pulp into a large mixing bowl, leaving a thin shell. Mash potatoes, adding salt, pepper, and margarine to taste and milk as needed. Stir in onion, cheddar and Jack cheeses, and spinach. Spoon potato mixture back into the shells.

Bake potato halves for 20 minutes or until lightly browned. Serve immediately. Or freeze potatoes before reheating them. To serve potatoes, remove as many as needed. Allow to thaw; place on a rimmed cookie sheet or in a baking dish. Bake in a preheated 400° oven about 20 minutes or until lightly browned. Makes 12 servings.

FRESH-BAKED ASPARAGUS

1 to 1½ pounds fresh asparagus
Salt and pepper to taste (lemon pepper, if desired)
3 tablespoons butter

*P*reheat oven to 300°. Rinse asparagus and trim off rough ends. Place spears in one or two layers in a baking pan. Sprinkle with salt and pepper, and dot with butter. Cover with foil and bake 30 minutes. The asparagus will be crunchy and will not lose color. Makes 6 to 8 servings.

MARINATED VEGGIES

Vegetables:
1 large stalk fresh broccoli
1 3½-ounce can medium pitted ripe olives, drained
1 16-ounce can green beans, drained
1 16-ounce can julienned carrots, drained
6 halved, cherry tomatoes
¼ pound sliced, fresh mushrooms

Marinade:
1 cup cider vinegar
1 cup vegetable oil
1 teaspoon minced garlic (1 large clove)
¾ teaspoon dried basil leaves
¾ teaspoon dried oregano leaves
¾ teaspoon salt
¼ teaspoon pepper
½ small onion, minced

*C*hop broccoli florets and a small portion of the upper stalk. Cook broccoli 5 minutes or until slightly crisp. Combine broccoli and remaining vegetables in a 2-quart casserole dish.

Mix marinade in a small saucepan, bring to a boil, reduce heat, and simmer for 10 minutes. Pour marinade over vegetables, toss, and refrigerate for several hours until chilled.

Note: Add your favorite cooked, small pasta for a Presto Pasta Salad.

MORE RECIPES — VEGETABLES

CHAPTER NINE
Adapting the Once-a-Month Cooking Method

*T*he eyes of all look to you,
and you give them their food at
the proper time. You open your
hand and satisfy the desires of
every living thing.

Psalm 145:15–16

CHOOSING RECIPES

Once you've tried once-a-month cooking, you may want to adapt it to your recipes. The following suggestions will help you set up your system.

Choose dishes that freeze well. (See the section on freezer storage tips in chapter 10.) Take into consideration that it's not safe to thaw meat, work with it, leave it raw, and then refreeze it. You must cook meat before freezing it again. But if you buy fresh meat, you can add ingredients and freeze the meat raw.

Start with your family's favorite recipes rather than exotic, new dishes. Or test recipes before you create your own plan. Be sure to pick simple recipes rather than ones that require many complicated steps. You need to keep your assembly order and food preparation as simple as possible. Otherwise, you'll be defeating your purpose of saving time.

Make sure you have a nice variety of recipes. You don't want to serve similar entrées too close together, such as two stews or three creamy noodle casseroles. If you don't mind eating the same dish twice in a month, double the recipe for a favorite entrée, divide it in half, and freeze it. You may also want to consider dishes that could be used for both lunch and dinner or could be taken to work and reheated in a microwave oven.

If you enjoy sharing food with others, choose some dishes that work well for company or could be taken to someone who is sick or has a special need.

After you decide what recipes you want to try, divide them into groups such as chicken, beef, fish, pork, meatless, or miscellaneous. This will show you how many recipes you have in each category. You may have too many chicken dishes or casseroles and need to balance your recipes by adding other kinds of meats or different types of dishes.

You may want to set up your system for only a week's worth of dishes rather than two weeks or a month. Or you may want to spread out the process, preparing all the dishes in a category at the same time—all the beef recipes in one afternoon, for example, and all the recipes in another category the next day.

Finally, make sure the ingredients called for in the recipes fit your budget. Some meats, especially fish, can be expensive.

MAKING A MENU CALENDAR

First, reproduce and use the blank calendar we've included in this chapter. Record recipes on it in pencil, in case you need to move them around.

Next, check your schedule for days the family will be away from home and won't need meals; cross off those dates. Take into account the nights you'll need to prepare something quick because you or your kids have meetings or activities. Pencil in easy-to-prepare dishes for those times. Make note of holidays or special occasions, such as birthdays or anniversaries, that will require special planning.

Organize your recipes by category, such as beef, chicken, or miscellaneous, before filling out the menu calendar. Make sure you will serve a variety of entrées for each week.

If you plan to have company, select the recipes you would use for the occasion, and write these entrées on the appropriate dates. Do the same with dishes you want to take to a friend or to a potluck. For dates when the adults will be away but the kids will be eating at home, choose dishes the children like and they or a babysitter can easily finish preparing.

If some dishes suit a particular day of the week, such as quiche on Sunday, add those recipes to the appropriate days. Then complete the calendar with your recipes.

Perhaps you may want to create your own plan without considering your schedule or special occasions. You just want to prepare two weeks or a month of meals at once and have them in your freezer. If you do that, you may still want to fill out a calendar so you have a variety of meals scheduled and as a way to keep track of the ones you've made. Check them off as you serve them to your family.

FIGURING SHOPPING AND STAPLES LISTS

Now use your recipes to compile your shopping and staples lists. You'll need a sheet of paper for each list. It may help to categorize your grocery list with the same headings we've used: Canned Goods; Grains, Pasta, and Rice; Dry Ingredients and Seasonings; Dairy Products; Meat and Poultry; and Produce.

You can also categorize your list by aisles or areas in your favorite supermarket. If you don't want to recopy your list, you can categorize by highlighting items with different-colored marking pens: pink for produce, brown for meat, green for canned goods, and yellow for bakery.

To figure what food you'll need, check ingredients in each recipe, and record all the items on either the grocery shopping or staples lists. For example, if a recipe calls for cinnamon and you already have it, put it on the staples list. But add it to the shopping list if you don't have it. If 2½ pounds of chicken pieces are required, put them on the shopping list. For items needed for more than one recipe, such as onions, ground beef, or tomato sauce, keep a running tally of quantities needed, and then figure the total. (See "Equivalent Measures" in chapter 10 for how to convert size of portions.)

Finally, be sure to list freezer bags or containers you will need in order to freeze each entrée. Then add the ones you'll need to your shopping list.

SETTING UP AN ASSEMBLY ORDER

Once you've filled in your calendar, check instructions in "The Day before Cooking Day" and "Cooking Day Assembly Order" for the two-week and one-month plans to help you make out your own assembly order.

Copy your recipes on large, blank index cards. Then spread the recipes on a table and arrange them in an order that will flow well when you're preparing them. Group recipes that use similar ingredients, particularly meats.

Once you have your recipes in order, go through each one, tallying the total amount of each food item you'll need to process: how many onions to chop, carrots to shred, or ground beef to brown.

When you write out the assembly order, try to work with two or three recipes in the same category at a time, such as all the ground beef recipes or all the chicken. Record all the ingredients you'll need to store or freeze until the accompanying dishes are served. List any tasks you'll need to do the day before cooking day, such as cooking all the chicken or soaking pinto beans. You may also want to plan to do most of the chopping, grating, shredding, and slicing tasks the day before cooking day.

Then make out an assembly order with directions for how to proceed from one recipe to the next. If you haven't scheduled the chopping and slicing tasks for the day before, plan to do them the first thing on cooking day. Recipes that require longer cooking, such as soups or stews, should also be started early in the day.

Make sure you'll have enough stove burners to cook dishes in a particular group at the same time. Whenever possible, combine steps for several dishes: cook rice for two dishes; sauté all onions at once.

Continue through all the recipes until you have completed your assembly order. Allow for time between groups of recipes so you can take some breaks.

CHAPTER NINE

EVALUATING YOUR PLAN

The first time you try your own plan, take a few extra minutes at the end to write out any corrections in the recipes or procedures. That way, the next time you cook, it will go even smoother.

The following suggestions will help you revise your plan:

❉ Correct the order of tasks if they weren't easy to follow or in the right order. If you would do any part of the procedure differently, state what you would do.

❉ If you should have prepared some dishes sooner or later in the process, make note of it.

❉ Rework your plan if you had too many or too few dishes to prepare at once.

❉ Write out new directions if they were difficult to follow in any of the sections.

❉ If needed, correct ingredients needed on your shopping list.

Menu

·CALENDAR·

Sunday	Monday	Tuesday	Wednesday	Thursday	Friday	Saturday
	1	2	3	4	5	6
7	8	9	10	11	12	13
14	15	16	17	18	19	20
21	22	23	24	25	26	27
28	29	30				

CHAPTER NINE

CHAPTER TEN
Special Helps

*A*nd if you spend yourselves
in behalf of the hungry and
satisfy the needs of the
oppressed, then your light
will rise in the darkness,
and your night will become
like the noonday.

Isaiah 58:10

EQUIVALENT MEASURES

1 tablespoon = 3 teaspoons or ½ fluid ounce

2 tablespoons = 1 fluid ounce

4 tablespoons = ¼ cup

5⅓ tablespoons = ⅓ cup

8 tablespoons = ½ cup

12 tablespoons = ¾ cup

16 tablespoons = 1 cup

1 cup = ½ pint or 8 fluid ounces

2 cups = 1 pint

2 pints = 1 quart

16 cups = 4 quarts or 1 liquid gallon

1 pound lean ground beef or sausage browned and drained = 2½ cups

1 pound cubed ham = 3 cups

1 cooked, deboned whole chicken (about 4 pounds) cooked and chopped = 4½ cups

1 pound boneless, skinless chicken cooked and chopped = 2¾ cups

1 medium yellow onion, chopped = 1¼ cups

1 medium yellow onion, chopped and sautéed = ¾ cup

1 medium green bell pepper, chopped = 1 cup

1 pound cheese, grated = 4 cups

3 ounces fresh mushrooms, sliced = 1 cup

1 pound zucchini, diced = 1½ cups

1 medium clove garlic, minced = 1 teaspoon

DEFINITIONS OF COOKING TERMS USED IN ONCE-A-MONTH COOKING

al dente - Slightly underdone with a chewy consistency, from the Italian phrase "to the tooth." Usually applied to the cooking of pasta, but can also apply to vegetables that are not fully cooked. Don't add pasta to water until it is rapidly boiling.

baste - To keep foods moist during cooking by spooning, brushing, or drizzling with a sauce or pan juice. A bulb baster is convenient to use (but practice with soapy water first before you try basting with hot liquids).

beat - To mix ingredients rapidly so that air is incorporated, resulting in a smooth, creamy mixture. A slightly beaten egg is a consistent, creamy yellow color.

blanch - To plunge vegetables, seafood, or fruit into rapidly boiling water for a brief period of time to bring out the color, preserve nutrients, loosen skins for peeling, or mellow flavor.

boil - To heat water or other liquids to 212° F at sea level. When water boils, its surface is covered with bubbles.

chop - To cut food into pieces, which can range from ½ inch (finely chopped) to 1 inch or more (coarsely chopped) in size. Makes pieces roughly uniform in size so they will cook more evenly.

dice - To cut into equal-size small cubes from ¼ inch to ½ inch. Cutting pieces uniformly in size makes them cook more evenly.

freezer burn - Food that has been left in a freezer too long and/or not sealed properly before freezing is said to have freezer burn. It is characterized by a blanket of ice crystals formed on the surface of the food and a "cardboard-like" taste. Such food should not make you sick, but is not pleasant to the taste. See freezing tips in this book (chapters 2 and 10) for preventative measures.

grate - To change a food's consistency to fine pieces by use of a grater or food processor. Shredding produces finer, thinner strands than does grating.

marinade/marinate - To tenderize and flavor food by placing it in a seasoned liquid usually composed of some combination of vinegar, lemon juice, oil, herbs, and/or spices.

mince - To cut or chop into very fine pieces, no larger than ⅛ inch square.

rare - Meat that has been cooked a short time to retain juices and tenderness. Rare meat will be brown on the outside but red in the center. The surest way to tell if meat is done is with a meat thermometer. If you cut into cooking meat to test for doneness, some of the juices will escape.

sauté - To cook food in butter or fat in a skillet until lightly browned. Sautéing is usually a quick process, so food should be sliced thin and should be tender. Don't brown garlic when you sauté it or it will turn bitter.

scald - To cook a liquid, most often milk or cream, over low heat until just before it boils. Look for small bubbles around the edge of the liquid.

SPECIAL HELPS

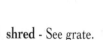
shred - See grate.

simmer - To cook liquid alone or along with other ingredients over low heat, never boiling. A few small bubbles may appear on the surface.

skim - To spoon off fat or scum that rises to the surface of a cooked liquid. May be done with a large spoon or baster.

zest - To remove in fine strips the outermost colored peel, or zest, of citrus fruits, being careful not to incorporate the bitter white pith just underneath the surface.

FOOD-HANDLING TIPS

You will work quickly on your cooking day, but don't neglect important precautions. Always wash your hands after handling eggs or poultry. Either use separate cutting boards for vegetables/fruits and meats/poultry, or wash cutting board thoroughly before switching from meats to vegetables.

MORE FREEZER STORAGE TIPS

Frozen foods keep their natural color, flavor, and nutritive qualities better than canned or dried foods. Freezing also stops the bacterial action in fresh food that causes it to spoil.

Food kept in the freezer too long may not taste right, but it shouldn't make you sick. However, it's not safe to thaw food, especially meat, and then refreeze it without first cooking it.

Freezing food in moisture-proof containers with airtight lids or seals will help it keep its color and flavor much longer. You'll get the best results with products made for freezer use: plastic containers with lids; heavy aluminum foil; heavy plastic bags; freezer wraps and tape. Glass jars with lids (leave head space for the food to expand when it freezes) also work well.

Avoid using regular waxed paper; lightweight aluminum foil; regular plastic wrap or cellophane; cartons from cottage cheese, ice cream, or milk; ordinary butcher paper; the plastic film used on packaged meats; or plastic produce bags from the supermarket.

Follow these helpful hints for freezing foods:

❋ Freeze food quickly to 0° or below.

❋ Post a dated list of food on the freezer door, and keep it current.

❋ Use frozen food within four to six weeks. Some seasonings become stronger while frozen, and some weaker. The degree of change is minimized if food is not left frozen too long.

* Thaw, heat, and serve food in rapid succession.
* Allow hot foods to cool to room temperature before freezing, then freeze them immediately.
* Blanch or precook vegetables and drain them before freezing to stop enzyme action and to keep them from becoming discolored and mushy. Drain blanched vegetables before freezing them.
* Thaw foods in the refrigerator or microwave whenever possible. Thawing in the refrigerator will take twice as long as on the counter, but it's much safer. Thawing time will vary according to the thickness or quantity of food in the container.
* So many foods freeze well that it's more helpful to ask what doesn't freeze well than what does. Don't freeze the following foods. They will change color, texture, or separate in some way during the freezing or thawing process:
    * Raw salad vegetables (such as lettuce, radishes, tomatoes).
    * Raw eggs in their shells or hard-cooked eggs.
    * Raw potatoes or boiled white potatoes (they turn black).
    * Commercial cottage cheese.
    * Gelatin salads or desserts.
    * Icing made with egg whites, boiled frostings, or cakes with cream fillings.
    * Instant rice (dissolves and becomes too mushy). You can freeze regular cooked rice.
    * Custard pies, cream pies, or pies with meringue.

USING THE COMPUTER

Based upon the book *Once-a-Month Cooking*, this CD-ROM, produced by Lifestyle Software Group, the industry leader in cookbook software, further streamlines the process for the busy family.

The program takes the once-a-month cooking method of cooking a month's dinner entrées (or two weeks' dinner entrées) in a day and freezing them, and simplifies the process with the aid of computer technology. The program takes the book's easy-to-follow meal plans and recipes, time-saving and freezer-storage tips, and grocery shopping strategies and adds video clips to the preparation guides. Unlike the book, the CD-ROM allows the cook to calculate the caloric and nutritional value of meals, adjust recipes to fit the number of portions desired, and print out recipes, shopping lists, and assembly orders.

SPECIAL HELPS

How can you add your own recipes to the Once-a-Month Cooking system on CD-ROM? Once you have used and grown comfortable with the Once-a-Month Cooking system on CD-ROM, you may adapt the system to your own recipes with the help of additional software, the Micro-Kitchen Companion by Lifestyle Software Group. You can scan or type in your own recipes, and the Micro-Kitchen Companion will generate your shopping list. You then must develop an assembly order, using tips from the CD-ROM as your guide.

System requirements: Microsoft Windows 3.1 or higher, Windows 95 compatible, 8 MG RAM, 8 MG hard disk space available, 2X CD-ROM or better, 16 bit sound.

The software is available at software outlets or by calling Lifestyle Software Group, 904-794-7070; E-mail: lsg@lifeware.com, Website: http://www.lifeware.com.

VIDEOS

A thirty-minute videotape of Mimi Wilson demonstrating the once-a-month cooking method is available for purchase or for a two-week rental. The video is helpful for those who need motivation to do once-a-month cooking or feel apprehensive about trying it, or to use as a program for women's groups.

A forty-five-minute videotape of Mimi Wilson speaking on The Ministry of Hospitality is also available. This tape is accompanied by a five-week study guide for use in Bible study groups. The video covers making use of available resources for hospitality, maintaining a welcoming attitude, involving children, understanding the differences between hospitality and entertainment, and discovering the rewards of being hospitable.

Please send videotape inquiries to Mardell Peterson, 305 W. Caley Circle, Littleton, Colorado 80120; phone (303) 794-2744; E-mail: marpete1@juno.com.

SPEAKING

Mimi Wilson and Mary Beth Lagerborg are available for speaking on The Once-a-Month Cooking Method and The Home as an Oasis. For information, contact Mardell Peterson at (303)794-2744.

INDEX

INDEX

C

INDEX

INDEX

INDEX